ENGLISH GLASS

ENGLISH
GLASS

Edited by Sydney Crompton
Contributors: E. M. Elville
Euan Ross

WARD LOCK LIMITED · LONDON

Second impression 1969
Third impression 1972

ISBN 0 7063 1029 2

Acknowledgements

The authors and publishers are indebted to the following for the use of illustrative material in this book.
British Museum 23, 28, 117; H. P. Bulmer & Co. Ltd.: Frontispiece; A. C. Burton 64, 65, 78, 87, 93, 111, 118, 119, 134, 138, 142, 147, 157, 158; Central Press Photos 19, 21; Arthur Churchill (Glass) Ltd. for most of the unlisted photographs; Corning Museum of Glass 3, 34; Cmnd A. O. Coxon: Front Cover, 151, 152, 153; Mr and Mrs A. G. Cranch 45; R. Dennis 76, 77, 79, 84, 90, 136, 141, 148, 154, 155, 165, 180; Glass Manufacturers' Federation 18, 20, 22, 160, 198, 202, 203; Dr D. L. Mackenzie 38, 40; R. L. Montgomery 41; Messrs Parkinson & Spencer Ltd. 15; Marjorie Parr 83, 105, 182, 193; R. D. Pilkington 33, 35, 38, 39, 45, 95, 102; Science Museum 16, 17; W. F. Smith, jnr. 47, 96; J. Strauss 7, 27, 31, 36, 59; Victoria and Albert Museum: Back Cover, 2, 4, 6, 10, 13, 57, 184, 185; Webb Corbett Ltd. 206; Whitefriars Glass 201, 204, 205.

Made and printed by
William Clowes & Sons, Limited
London, Beccles and Colchester

Set in Monotype Ehrhardt

CONTENTS

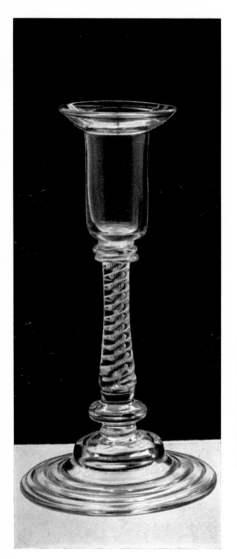

PLATE 1   A fine, rare candlestick, the nozzle collared at the
base. The stem contains a multi-
ply spiral opaque white twist
surrounded by a dark blue spiral
and an outer two-ply spiral band,
and has an annular knop at the
base. Domed and terraced foot.
8 ins. high. Circa 1760.

I

THE TRADITIONS OF ENGLISH GLASS

Viewed as a part of the whole history of glassmaking, the production of glass in England at the hands of Englishmen is only a recent innovation. For there is no record of any glass being found in England that pre-dates the Romans, and most of the glass that was manufactured here before the 17th century was produced by foreign workmen. In the once-fertile lands beside the Nile the story is a much longer one, and the remains of a glass furnace at Tell-el-Amarna show that glassmaking was already an industry in Egypt in about 1370 B.C. The origins of the industry go even further back, to a moulded amulet of deep *lapis lazuli* colour, dated about 7000 B.C., the oldest known piece of pure glass, and to the green glaze on stone beads of about 12000 B.C. At this distance of time we can no longer hope to identify with certainty the place where glass was first produced, but the evidence seems to point to Asia Minor, particularly Mesopotamia, and to suggest that the Egyptians under the powerful Pharaohs of the 18th dynasty imported both glass and glassmakers from this area. As for how glassmaking was discovered this is even more obscure, though Pliny's story of its accidental discovery by the fusion of sand and soda in an open fire is not unlikely, as glass certainly can be produced in this way.

Before glassmaking had become an established industry in England, most of the techniques of glass production and decoration had already been discovered and used in other countries. The

PLATE 2   Large jug, the globular body with moulded flutes on a ring foot. Found in a grave at Old Newington, near Stowmarket, Suffolk. Roman glass of the 2nd century A.D.

Egyptians found a way of producing hollow glass vessels, like unguent jars and vases, by winding threads of glass round a core of sand built up on a metal rod, or by dipping the core into a pot of glass several times, building up the layers of glass. When the glass had cooled, the core could be removed. Bowls and dishes they made by pressing glass into open moulds, and vases were decorated with bright looped patterns, achieved by applying tiny coloured glass threads to the vase, softening them by reheating, and pulling them into patterns. By the 2nd century B.C. the Egyptian glass industry was highly sophisticated, and could fulfill very ambitious orders. A dinner service of 150 pieces in transparent yellowish-white glass is a good example.

The greatest single advance in glass technology was the invention of blown glass, which probably took place in Syria in about 50 B.C. At first the glass was blown into a mould, but it was only a short step to the technique of free-blowing which made it possible to shape a piece of glass into almost any form. Later, the hollow rods which were used for glass-blowing were lengthened making it possible to blow the glass at a higher temperature and to mix the ingredients more thoroughly.

The dominion of the Romans meant that glass became available in every part of the Roman Empire, and the Romans themselves freely adopted the techniques that had been discovered by others. Glass was exported from Egypt and Syria to distant places, and men like Frontinus of Picardy learned the techniques of the Egyptians in order to produce glass in their own country. This remains the greatest period that glass has known, because of the tremendous variety of techniques used and the amazingly creative spirit that inspired the Roman glassmakers. Their achievements varied from the white and rich-blue cameo vase found in the tomb of Alexander Severus, which we call the 'Portland Vase', to the 'Lycurgus Cup', also in the British Museum, an example of the *diatreta* technique by which beakers and cups were decorated with carved ornament that seems to float above their surfaces. Other technical innovations resulted in the *millefiori* vessels, decorated with hundreds of rods of coloured glass fused together, and the *schmelzglas* that imitated marble. The Syrians used the *semé d'or* technique to give their glass a golden shimmer, blew bottles in the shape of Janus heads, and added beautiful, painted designs; while the Egyptians showed a liking for colour, especially blue, green, and amber, which they used on a wide variety of objects.

We are fortunate that so much Roman glass has survived. The glass that was much used at late Roman banquets was unfortunately destroyed at once, but many other items were buried with the dead and have been preserved. They have even improved with burial in many cases, for the action of the soil has caused the surface of the glass to deteriorate, and the refraction of light off this surface produces a brilliant iridescent effect. After the end of the 4th century there are much fewer specimens, for Christianity put an end to the pagan grave-burials. Very little is known about the late Roman glass industry, apart from the probability that the Roman glassmakers followed Constantine to Byzantium when he made that city the centre of the Empire in A.D. 330, and continued to produce vessels in much the same style until they came under the influence of Islam.

The Romans certainly imported glass into England from Egypt, Syria, and Gaul during their term of occupation, and there is also some evidence that, as in other northern European countries, native glass was produced by Roman-trained craftsmen. What appear to be the remains of glassworks from this period can be seen at Wilderspool near Warrington, at Castor in Northamptonshire, and at Colchester, and, according to Pliny the naturalist, glass was imported into England in lumps for remelting, colouring, and working into shapes by British glassmen. But it seems certain that if the Britons did make glass, the production did not continue for long after the departure of the Romans. Bede (673–735) tells us that Benedict Biscop, Abbot of Wearmouth and Jarrow, 'sent emissaries to Gaul to bring back glassmakers, craftsmen indeed till then unknown to the British, to furnish with glass the lattice-work shutters of his Churches and the windows of his cloisters and upper rooms. They not only fulfilled

PLATE 3 'Anglo-Saxon' beaker of free-blown olive-green glass in the form of an elongated cone with slightly everted rim. Said to have been found in a Yorkshire grave towards the end of the 19th century. Post-Roman, 5th century A.D.

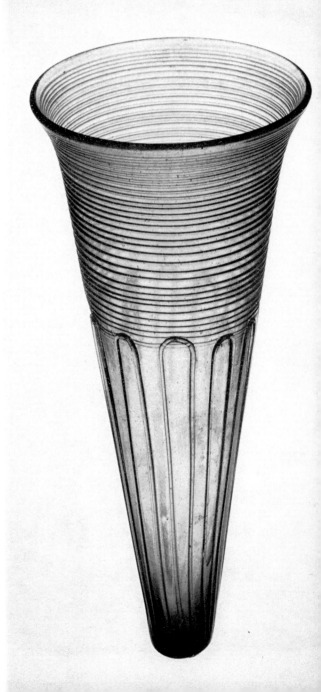

their contract, but also consequently caused the English to acquire this craft.' Apparently the English soon forgot what they had learnt, for in the 8th century Cuthbert of Jarrow was writing to the Bishop of Mainz for glassworkers, 'seeing that of that art we are ignorant and without resource'. We must conclude that the early attempts to make the English into glassmakers were not successful, and that the possession of delicate material such as glass was not altogether to the taste of a rude people whose lives were constantly being disrupted by the successive invasions of Saxons, Danes, and Norwegians. 'Anglo-Saxon' glass has been found in England, but it is in all cases so similar to the greenish *waldglas* of Germany or *verre de fougère* of France, and it comes in shapes so like those of the northern European glasses – cone-beakers and *Russelbecher* – that it cannot be taken as proof of native production.

It is only in the 13th century that the history of English glass begins to take shape and to be clothed in fact rather than conjecture. In 1226, one Laurence Vitrearius ('Laurence the Window-glass Maker') arrived in England from Normandy, equipped with the knowledge needed to make *verre de fougère* – 'bracken glass' in which the constituent potash was supplied by burnt bracken. He settled down to manufacture glass at Dyer's Cross, near Chidding-fold, by the Surrey-Sussex border, and it is known that other immigrants also came to the Weald of Surrey, Sussex, and Kent with the same idea in mind. Laurence's success in producing window-glass by the 'crown' method (in which the mark where the blowpipe is cast off is allowed to remain) is witnessed by the fact that by about 1240 he was making glass for Westminster Abbey. His son, William le Verrir, was also a successful glassmaker, and it must have been partly because of his good work that Chiddingfold received a royal charter in 1300. But what is most important about Laurence and his son is that they seem at last to have founded a permanent glass industry in the Weald, which lasted in the hands of their successors until the early 17th century. Their immediate 14th-century successors, John de Alemayen and Richard Holmere, continued to provide greenish-white window-glass for ecclesiastical buildings, and also to

PLATE 4 Window-glass from Winchester College Chapel. The subjects are: St. John the Evangelist, St. James the Less, and the prophet Ezekiel. English. Circa 1399.

make 'urynalls, bottles, bowles, cuppis to drinck, and such lyke' for the people of the immediate neighbourhood, and John Schurterre, who later bought Alemayen's factory at Fromes, also produced some vessel-glass in addition to his main concern of making glass for windows. Not that there was not plenty for the window-glass maker to do in this period when the lighter Gothic style provided a much larger amount of space for glazing than had the early Norman buildings. In Chiddingfold itself there were other manufactories, notably that of the Dedyngtons, who made glass for the newly founded Winchester College and New College, Oxford, and window-glass was also being made in Oxfordshire, Gloucestershire, and Staffordshire. The variety of vessel-glass may have been considerable, but very little has survived save for a few drinking-glasses, lamps, and bottles, all in a greenish metal, some of which were free-blown and others made in moulds.

In the mid-16th century another group from abroad came to England to manufacture glass. These were Huguenots from Lorraine and Normandy who had left their country partly because of religious persecution, and partly because there was already overproduction of glass in Lorraine. They were introduced into England by 'the astute Antwerp promoter' John Carré, who, in 1567, petitioned Queen Elizabeth for a monopolistic licence to make vessel-glass in the Venetian style in London. The monopoly was refused, but instead, in an attempt to revive the moribund English window-glass industry, Carré was granted a licence to make 'glas for glasinge', on condition that he paid a royalty for his monopoly and trained Englishmen in the art. Carré experienced some difficulty in obtaining wood – the competition of the iron-founders was already making things difficult for the glassmen – but eventually set up his factory in the Surrey–Sussex area like his predecessors, and also succeeded in founding a crystal-glass factory run by Lorrainers in London, to which he imported, for the first time in English history, the soda needed for the manufacture of Venetian glass. Other Lorrainers and Normans also looked beyond the bounds of the Weald for a better situation, encouraged by the wood shortage, and moved to Hampshire and later to Gloucestershire and North Staffordshire, producing glasses in a pale green metal in styles similar to those of the Netherlands and the Rhine – phials, ribbed flasks, and drinking-glasses of beaker shape or following styles set by the Venetians.

Carré had introduced some Venetian glassmakers into his Crutched Friars factory in London, and, ironically, it was one of these, Jacopo Verzelini (1522–1606), who eventually obtained the monopoly that Carré himself had been seeking. In 1575, Elizabeth granted him a 21-year privilege for the making of Venice glass in England, and, to assure his success, the import of Venetian glasses was forbidden and those who dared to infringe the monopoly were liable to fines of ten shillings per glass or £200 per furnace. It is not known how many glasses Verzelini produced or in what variety he made them. He may have manufactured all kinds of bowls and dishes that have with time become confused with true Venetian glass or Netherlandish glass, but the only pieces that have certainly been ascribed to him are a series of goblets, with hollow, moulded or gadrooned knops in the stem. One bears a gilded pattern damaged by time, but most of the others are engraved in diamond-point. The subject-matter of the decoration varies from the continuous hunting scene of the 1577 glass to the two glasses of 1583 and 1586 which carry the motto of the Pewterers' Company of London – 'In God is al mi trust'.

Verzelini retired in 1592, and the remainder of his privilege was taken over by Sir Jerome Bowes, soldier and company promoter. Only a single complete specimen of his glass remains – a wineglass in the Venetian style, not dissimilar to Verzelini's glasses, with 'Barbara Potters' engraved on it in diamond-point.

By the beginning of the 17th century the problem of fuel for the glass furnaces had become acute. In spite of the system of monopolies, wandering glassmakers continued to turn out window-glass and small objects in the common green glass of the Middle Ages for the use of ordinary people. While they were using up the country woods, the big patentees were trying to find ways of replacing wood by coal. In 1615, Sir Robert Mansell who, as a retired admiral, had a

PLATE 5 This glass was almost certainly made in one of the London glasshouses run by Jacopo Verzelini, and may have been decorated by Anthony de Lysle. The bowl decoration includes the arms of the Vintners' Company, the name *Wenyfrid Geares*, and the date 1590. Unfortunately, the gilding is now very much worn. This glass is the only known piece by Verzelini to be decorated in gilt. Of the other nine recorded, seven are engraved in diamond-point and two are neither decorated nor dated.

PLATE 6   Verzelini goblet engraved in diamond-point. The
decoration includes a stag and a unicorn pursued by two
hounds, separated by single trees; a border of arabesque
foliage broken by three bracket panels containing in hatched
characters (a) *John* and *Jone*, (b) *Dier* and *1591*, (c) the Royal
Arms as borne by Queen Elizabeth; a border of hatched
gadroons. The foot also decorated with a border of hatched
gadroons. A marriage glass.

2—E.G.

special interest in the preservation of the remaining woods for ship-building, joined with one Thomas Percival, who was supposed to have perfected a method of using coal in the glass furnaces, forming a new company and obtaining by 1623 the sole right to make 'all manner of drinking glasses, window glasses, looking glasses and all other kinds of glasses, bugles, bottles, vials or vessels whatever'. With his technical knowledge, Mansell could not fail, for in 1615 a royal proclamation had banned the use of wood in glassmaking, destroying the small-time glassmaker and depriving the ordinary people of the common, domestic glass. The luxury trade, on the other hand, boomed, and the Venetian ambassador in London wrote that, thanks to the training of Englishmen by Venetian glassmakers in London and Newcastle, 'there are many English who work admirably, and the crystal obtains a beauty not sensibly inferior but of quite equal quality to that of Murano, which used to have the pre-eminence and was the pride of all the world'. After his death, Mansell's monopolistic tradition was carried on by the Duke of Buckingham, who had a patent for a glasshouse at Greenwich, held the sole privilege for making 'mirror-plate' in his Vauxhall factory, and also controlled the patents granted to three other crystal-glass makers.

It is probable that both Mansell and Buckingham continued to produce glasses in the Venetian style, but without the Venetian ornament. Mansell, like his predecessors, employed Italian glass-makers, especially those from l'Altare in Montferrat, near Genoa, and Buckingham employed Venetians at Greenwich. John Greene, the glass-seller, reported in 1672 that the English glasses were more easily broken than the true Venetian products. Probably English specimens do survive, but have long been thought to be Venetian. It is John Greene himself who provides us with the clearest idea of what style was popular in England at this period, for when the English manufacture was interrupted by the Civil War he asked the Venetian Morelli to make some glasses for him to designs which he enclosed. These included wineglasses with flat-based inverted conical bowls and short knopped stems, versions of the German

The Traditions of English Glass

roemer, cylindrical tumblers, and covered goblets with 'ears', some in milk-white glass or speckled emerald glass.

The prohibition of 1615 had not completely destroyed the manufacture of common glass. Phials and medicine bottles continued to be made, and the first serving-bottle for wine, or bottle-decanter, appeared in about 1623. The latter was used both to bring wine from the vintner to the house (the vintner corked it lightly, tying the cork down with a thread which ran under the string-rim, situated just below the orifice) and for service at table. The metal used was a blackish-green or dark brown, and the development in styles of bottle can be traced thanks to the common practice of adding a date, initials, and some arms or a device of some sort to a pad on the shoulder of the bottle. Much of this trade was the responsibility of the Glass Sellers' Company who received a charter for this kind of work in 1635.

With the Restoration there began a new era in glassmaking, during which both the metal and the styles employed were modified, producing at last a distinctively English fashion in glasses. Neri, in his *L'Arte Vetraria*, had asserted that glass of lead was 'as to colour the finest and noblest glass', and when this important work was translated into English in 1662 by Christopher Merret the translator commented, 'tis a thing unknown in our furnaces, and the reason is because of the exceeding brittleness thereof'. Fourteen years later lead glasses were being produced in England of startlingly high quality, thanks to the work of George Ravenscroft (1618–81), who became official glassmaker to the Glass Sellers' Company in 1674. Ravenscroft's early metal was called 'flint-glass', probably because he was obtaining the required silica from English flints instead of the usual Venetian stones. They produced a less fusible kind of silica, while an increase in the fusibility of the materials was already needed now that the glasspots had to be closed to keep out sulphurous coal fumes. Finding that excessive use of alkali, in the form of potash, though making the materials more fusible, also produced 'crizz-ling' – a fine network of cracks in the interior of the finished glass – Ravenscroft substituted an oxide of lead called litharge for a proportion of the alkali. The final material this produced, though heavier than Venetian glass, had a brilliance and a light-dispersing quality unmatched by any previous manufacture, and during the next 50 years English glass, and especially wineglasses, went through a period that has not since been matched in its perfect combination of inventiveness, restraint, and fine metal.

Ravenscroft remedied the crizzling defect in his flint-glasses in 1676 and continued to produce glass at the Savoy glasshouse until his death in 1681, though he handed over the experimental glasshouse at Henley-on-Thames to Hawley Bishopp. He distinguished his own productions for the Glass Sellers' Company by means of a raven's head seal, and glassmakers in general used seals from about 1684 onwards. Ravenscroft's technical achievement gave a new impetus to glass production all over the country, and by the end of the century there were glasshouses in Stourbridge, South Shields, Newcastle-on-Tyne, and Bristol, to name only a few. Stylistically, the soda-glass goblets with hollow baluster stems of the mid-17th century were succeeded by a fashion for short stems with 'wrought buttons', which in turn gave way to more simplified forms with solid stems and the fine proportion associated with all the artistic productions of Queen Anne's reign.

The Baluster Period in wineglasses began in the late 17th century and lasted well into the 18th century. Its main features were: the use of contrasting discs and globular, cylindrical, urn-shaped or true baluster knops in the stem, the length of the stem being, at first, rather less than the height of the bowl, though during the reign of George I it was lengthened in proportion to the bowl; in the early period, straight-sided funnel-shaped bowls, becoming waisted and flared under George I; and a foot which was almost flat at the beginning of the period, but which gradually became more and more dome-like in the centre. In the early glasses, the knops might be lobed, ribbed, gadrooned, 'wrythen' (decorated with spiral reeding), or pincered, and the lower part of the bowl might also be gadrooned or wrythen. The stem contained a single air-bubble, which in the later glasses was replaced by a cluster of small air-bubbles or beads.

The Traditions of English Glass

The second important style of the early 18th century involved the so-called Silesian stem, a ribbed and shouldered stem in fact derived from the Hessian and West German styles which began to interest the English manufacturers at about the time of George I's arrival from Hanover. Later developments of this style produced reeded or polygonal stems, often twisted spirally and surrounded by a ring of bosses. These styles were of course applied to other objects apart from wineglasses. There were salvers with baluster or Silesian stems, and candlesticks, too, comprised stem and foot motifs similar to those used on the glasses.

The introduction of the excise duty on glass in 1745/6, which was based on the weight of the materials used, rapidly put an end to a style which was based on the generous use of heavy lead metal. The new styles were lighter, the metal used more watery as the lead content was reduced, and the accent was on the decoration of the glass rather than on the perfection of its form. Both cutting and engraving took a new lease of life. Little of the early cut-glass survives, probably because much of it was destroyed and used as 'cullet' when the cost of materials was increased by the excise duty, but the sweetmeat glasses and cruet bottles that have survived are scalloped and faceted in the manner of the contemporary English mirror glass. Wheel-engraving became popular with the 'flowered glasses' of the early 1740's, and unpretentious and modestly executed borders of scrollwork, flowers, vine leaves and grapes are perhaps the most characteristic English engraved work of this period, especially on light baluster glasses with waisted or ogee bowls or on the drawn-stem glasses (in which the bowl was drawn out to form a stem) with trumpet bowls. The finest wheel-engraving on English glasses took place abroad, especially in the Netherlands. As even the best of Dutch glasses were lightweight and dull compared with the English glasses, most of the high-quality glasses with Dutch engraving are of English manufacture, a large proportion of them from Newcastle. Some of them are in styles not commonly seen in England, and were probably made specially for the Dutch market.

Newcastle was also the home of many of the air-twist glasses which

PLATE 7 A large, Anglo-Venetian goblet. The bowl is related to the Venetian style, but the stem is typically English. The new lead-glass required simpler and heavier forms than the flexible soda-glass of Murano. $11\frac{3}{4}$ ins. high. Circa 1685.

became popular in the middle of the century, and which were advertised in 1737 as 'wormed' or 'wrought' glasses. The decorative corkscrew and criss-cross patterns were achieved by elongating and twisting a lump of glass containing air-bubbles and forming it into a drawn or knopped stem, or later a straight stem. In the late 1740's manufacturers started to make similar patterns with opaque white or coloured glass threads in the stem, a technique derived from the Venetian *latticinio*. These 'enamel-twists', as we call them, became fashionable in the late 1750's and 1760's, and, at the same time, another Venetian technique, that of external spiral reeding, was revived in the form of 'incised twist' glasses.

The middle of the century saw a great variety in bowl formations. There were funnel-shaped bowls that became more slender as the century progressed; small 'bucket'-shaped bowls; waisted 'thistle'-shaped bowls; ogee bowls; and the ever-popular drawn stem and bowl shape. Long straight stems were the fashion, though some large bowls were produced on baluster stems, and the 'Hogarth' glasses had almost no stem at all.

Many of the political events of the 18th century, from local elections to the Seven Years War, were recorded in diamond-point engraving on glasses, very often in an amateurish style, and frequently on Newcastle glasses. The most highly sought-after of these are the Jacobite and Williamite glasses, which were purchased in token of loyalty to the Stuart cause and the descendants of James II or to the Hanoverian successors of William of Orange. The rarest and most precious of these are the 'Amen' glasses, which bear the cipher IR, direct and reversed, and the figure 8 (i.e. Jacobus Rex VIII, meaning James Francis Edward Stuart, the Old Pretender) followed by two or more verses of the Jacobite hymn ending with the word *Amen*. These glasses would have been made for certain important Jacobites, who were probably personally acquainted with James. He and his son, Charles, are both recorded by their pretended titles ('God Save the King, I Pray' 'God Bliss the Prince of Wales'), while Charles's brother Henry is recorded by name, presumably out of courtesy, for Henry had contracted out of the competition for the

English throne by assuming a cardinalship in 1747. It is unlikely that the glasses were made before that date. The similarity between the engraving suggests that they were all engraved at about the same time, two of them bear the date 1749, and two others are of about 1750. The style of the glasses, which are mainly drawn stem or baluster type, some with air-twist stems, is of no help in dating, as the engraving could have been done long after their manufacture, and even the dates engraved on them are no sure guide, as they, too, could have been added. As for where these glasses were engraved, the use of 'Bliss' for 'Bless', and the number eight in Arabic instead of Roman numerals, has been taken to suggest Scotland, and most of the 'Amen' glasses certainly were in the possession of Scottish families.

The 'Amen' glasses were probably the most exclusive of the Jacobite glasses, but as the plausibility of the Jacobite cause decreased so the output of Jacobite glasses in token of loyalty seems to have increased, and many specimens have survived which date from the 20-year period that followed the disaster of Culloden Moor. The throne of England was commonly represented by an engraved Rose, and James and Charles by Rosebuds. In the early period there was a single unopened bud on the sinister side, which represented the Old Pretender, but in the hopeful period between 1741 and 1745, when the Young Pretender also became known to his followers, James was represented on the dexter side by an opening bud, and Charles by a closed bud on the other side. There was no need to change this until 1766 when the Old Pretender died, and then his bud was merely removed from the design, which therefore became identical with the designs on the pre-1741 glasses. Of the other Jacobite glasses, probably few were engraved before 1746. Some of them bore Jacobite slogans: *Fiat; Redeat; Revirescit; Health to all our fast friends; Success to the Society* (meaning the Society of Jesus); etc. Others were engraved with portraits of Charles Edward, and occasionally of his father, and there were other symbols used apart from the Rose. The Thistle was used to represent the Scottish Crown; the Star, to signify Jacobite endeavour; the Oak Leaf could

PLATE 8 Wineglass, the round funnel bowl on a double-knopped, multiple-spiral air-twist stem and plain circular foot. The bowl is engraved with a Jacobite rose and a single bud joined to a thistle. On reverse, a prince's coronet on which stands a lion, full-faced, wearing a Royal Crown (the crest of a younger son or brother of a sovereign of Great Britain). $6\frac{1}{2}$ ins. high. Circa 1750.

either mean restoration to the English throne, from its association with the Boscobel Oak of Charles II, or was a symbol for mourning; the Stricken Oak was the unlucky House of Stuart, and bore in addition two sprouting leaves, or one or two saplings. The meaning of the Compass and of the Daffodil is rather obscure, and the Forget-me-not could have a number of meanings, but the insect which appears on a number of the glasses, whether it be moth, butterfly, bee, or just an indeterminate insect, has been interpreted as an attempt to represent the return of the exiled soul to its native Scotland after death. This is credible on the single-budded glasses made after the death of James, but when both Pretenders were alive it seems to be a very despairing motif to use.

The opposing Williamite glasses were engraved with such symbols as Orange Trees, and Irish Harps, and there were also portraits, especially equestrian portraits, of William III. The glasses made in the Seven Years War (1756–63) bore engravings of ships or privateers, and portraits of Frederick the Great or Britannia, together with patriotic mottos. It should be added that few of these glasses, including the Jacobite glasses, showed a very high standard of engraving.

In the middle of the century, glass enamelling came into favour, notably in the work of the Beilby family on Newcastle glass, and in the enamelling done by a number of artists on the glass that has acquired the name 'Bristol', which we may take as a generic rather than a geographical title. William Beilby (1740–1819) and Mary Beilby (1749–97) were son and daughter of a goldsmith, and were probably helped in their work by their brother, Ralph, a silversmith, and by Thomas Bewick, his apprentice. Most of their work is done in a bluish- or pinkish-white monochrome, and their designs often included birds, especially peacocks, landscapes with obelisks and ruins, growing vines, electioneering appeals, depictions of rural pastimes, scrollwork, and naturalistic flowers and fruit, and some armorial glasses were also enamelled by William. Their first designs were executed about 1762 or 1763, and the series continued until 1778 when, after the death of their mother, both William and Mary left Newcastle to settle down in Fife.

PLATE 9 Baluster stem glasses. *Left*: Wineglass with drawn round funnel bowl. The inverted baluster stem has a small tear and a base knop. High conical folded foot. $5\frac{1}{4}$ ins. high. Circa 1700. *Right*: Wineglass. The round funnel bowl is on a cushion knop over a flat knop, a squat inverted baluster, and a base knop. High conical folded foot. $5\frac{1}{4}$ ins. high. Circa 1720.

The Traditions of English Glass

The revived taste for porcelain in England, and the fact that 'enamel glass' was not included in the Excise Act until 1777, encouraged the production of an opaque white glass, similar in appearance to porcelain and often painted by the same people who decorated porcelain or in a similar style. This glass is generally called 'Bristol', and may actually have originated in Bristol for we know that one Jacob Little, a member of a Stourbridge family, had a 'white flint glasshouse' in Bedminster as early as 1752. But it was also produced elsewhere. There are bottles to be found with the names of the condiments on them in Dutch which were most certainly made in Newcastle though the metal is 'Bristol', and there are 'Bristol' scent-bottles whose style of enamelling, gilding, and faceting has suggested to some that they are the work of the Birmingham and South Staffordshire boxmakers. The glass was much used for trumpet-mouthed beakers, covered vases, four-sided tea-caddies, cream jugs, patch stands, sugar bowls, and candlesticks with reeded stems. Many of the pieces are decorated with naturalistic birds and bunches of flowers, scrollwork, or *chinoiserie*, usually painted in oil or varnish and fired to hold the colour, though sometimes transfer printing was used. The standard of painting varies, not surprisingly, for though some of the pieces were painted by professional artists like Michael Edkins, who worked for a number of opaque-glass manufacturers in Bristol, others were painted by 'home painters', who bought the finished glasses from the factories and decorated them at home before selling them to the shops.

The same period also saw the production of the famous blue glass which is also associated with Bristol and was certainly made there early in its history. Michael Edkins recorded how he enamelled cans and beakers of blue glass when he was employed by Lazarus Jacobs in Bristol. The colouring of this rich, dark-blue glass was achieved by the use of smalt, which was imported from Saxony into the port of Bristol, and it was probably the fact that the glassmakers had to go to Bristol to obtain this constituent, rather than any local specialisation, that gave rise to the name 'Bristol Blue'. Toilet-bottles, scent-bottles, and patch-boxes are found in blue glass, but the decanters are

PLATE 10 Large sealed wine-bottle. While English crystal
was developing, common green glass continued to be made
in forms derived from Roman glass. Early 18th century.

probably the most striking pieces, especially those with the names of drinks gilded on them, or engraved on gilt labels suspended from their necks by means of gilt chains. Some of the pieces are facet cut, or, like the perfume- and snuff-bottles, painted with delightful scenes, and amethyst purple and emerald-green glass was also used for all sorts of objects from drinking-glasses to rolling-pins.

Cut-glass continued in popularity from the mid-18th century onwards, and, as well as scalloping and slicing, patterns were built up from a series of facets or 'hollow diamonds'. 'Diamond-cut scalloped candlesticks' were being advertised as early as 1742, and diamond-faceted stems were still being used for wineglasses during the classical period set in motion by Robert Adam towards the end of the century. The light-dispersing qualities of lead-glass have already been mentioned, and, when it was discovered how much cutting enhanced this quality, cut-glass naturally began to be used for candlesticks and chandeliers. Before 1750, chandeliers were made in the Palladian style commonly used in the brass chandeliers of the time, with plain arms and delicate hollow diamond-cutting in the shaft pieces, but as the century progressed more and more decoration was applied – canopies at the top and base, hung with pendant lustres, in the 1750's and 1760's; and extravagant rococo ornament in the 1760's and 1770's. During the 1770's the Adam style dictated a classical urn in place of the heavy cut-glass ball in the shaft, and the irregular-shaped pendant drops were replaced by pendant pear-shaped drops and delicate glass spires pointing upwards. By the turn of the century the accent was on an overall profusion of pendant lustres, and as the 19th century progressed the shaft was completely obscured by a shower of cut drops.

While the excise duty in England was progressively increased in 1771, 1781, and 1787, there was no excise duty on Irish glass until 1825, and the advantages of manufacturing glass in Ireland became clear when free trade was granted between the two countries in 1780 and the taste for deep cutting revived in England. Many English designers and glassmakers moved over to Ireland, and the Waterford factory, for example, was an offshoot of the Stourbridge industry.

PLATE 11 Both sides of a wine decanter, the spire stopper
cut with shallow diamonds. Enamelled and signed *Beilby
inv & pinx*. On the neck is a butterfly, much used by the
Beilbys as a decorative motif. Circa 1770.

The Traditions of English Glass

The style the Anglo-Irish industry developed was composed of heavy classical shapes, decorated with deep and extensive cutting, and, as well as using all the earlier techniques used in England, the cutters added 'prismatic ridges', created by cutting deep, parallel grooves, and 'raised diamonds' in high relief, which were often criss-crossed or cut with stars to form 'strawberry diamonds'. The range of items included decanters, wine-coolers, goblets, fruit-bowls, and massive urn-shaped vases.

Perhaps the most delightful consequence of the oppressive excise duty on glass was the encouragement it gave to the manufacture of the glass we know as Nailsea, originally at Nailsea near Bristol and later in Birmingham and other parts of the country as well. In 1788 the bottle-maker J. R. Lucas began to make domestic vessels in bottle glass because the excise was lower, and from 1810 to 1815 his Nailsea works were managed by R. L. Chance, who employed John Hartley of Dumbarton, a leading expert on glass manufacturing, in 1812. Under Chance, the Nailsea industry was at its most creative. Two main sorts of decoration were used: the *latticinio* or ribbon effect, which was probably the work of the French glassmakers who lived in 'French Rank' in Nailsea; and the splashing and flecking of the greenish-black bottle-glass with white, opaque white, pale golden brown, yellow, dark red, pink and salmon, and a variety of greens and blues. Both techniques were used on the characteristic Nailsea flasks, which are said to have been sometimes used by those leisured ladies and gentlemen who came to take the waters at Bath. There were hollow glass balls smeared with bright colours inside, and calculated to deflect the Evil Eye. There were rolling-pins with knops at each end and one end open, suitable for keeping flour or smuggling liquor if corked. There were the jugs whose predominant metal might be black, greenish-black, brownish-claret, pale green, or amber, flecked with an inexhaustible range of colours. There were bells, model bellows, glass paperweights and tobacco pipes, and, most eccentric of all, there were the pieces of long glass which George Soane noticed in Devon and recorded in his *Curiosities of Literature* (1847): 'The most curious of their general superstitions is that of the glass rod, which they set up clean in their houses, and wipe clean every morning, under the idea that all diseases from malaria will gather about the rod innoxiously. It is twisted in the form of a walking stick, and is from 4 to 8 feet long.'

In spite of the metal used, the Nailsea glass was quite sophisticated compared with some of the country glass, made for selling in country markets and fairs, which was produced elsewhere, epecially in the Midlands and the North. These cups, jugs and vases in blue, green, or purple, often bore mottos like: 'Be canny with the cream.' Mottos, sentimental, religious or moralistic, and flowers painted in unfired colours were a feature too of the watery opal-white glass, like debased 'Bristol', in which milk-jugs, vases, and rolling-pins were made, though the work of the early 19th-century enameller Absolon of Yarmouth is quite distinctive. Mention should also be made of the doorstops, associated with Kilner's Wakefield factory, made with green bottle-glass enclosing plant-like designs covered with air-bubbles.

As the 19th century progressed, new techniques were discovered, old techniques were revived and combined, and glass began to be made by machinery as well as by craftsmen. The Victorian glass-makers and glassbuyers must have been highly impressionable, to judge from the ephemeral life-span of the successive new styles, and it would be a very long book that took account of all the fashions in 19th-century glass. We must confine ourselves here to a few general remarks.

Cut-glass remained in favour with the middle classes until the 1850's, and was revived in the 1880's and 1890's. The styles of cut-glass from 1830 onwards were recorded by Samuel Miller, the fore-man cutter at the Waterford works, and we can see from his patterns how decanters, for example, became heavier, passing from cylindrical shapes and 'Gothic' patterns to globular shapes cut with 'printies' or shallow hollows. The removal of the glass excise in 1845 made possible the heavy fluting and deep cutting that reached its peak in the exhibits displayed at the Great Exhibition in 1851, and fan-scalloping and radial stars under decanter bases became popular. It

PLATE 12 *Left*: Tumbler engraved *E. & M. Howarth 1840* within foliage. 4⅛ ins. high. *Right*: Tumbler engraved with a pillared archway bearing the words *God is Our Guide Brotherly Love*, and a number of Masonic emblems. 4⅜ ins. high. Circa 1840.

The Traditions of English Glass

was not Ruskin's condemnation of all cut-glass as 'barbaric' that put it out of fashion, but the success of the technique of press-moulding, which had been rediscovered in America in the 1820's. In Britain, very passable glasses in imitation of cut-glass styles were produced for the less affluent, and it was not until the 1870's, when cut-glass was out of fashion, that stippled grounds and patterns and commemorative inscriptions in raised dots gave a distinctive style to pressed glass.

The enthusiasm for coloured glass, which had been current in Bohemia since the 1820's, suddenly became a feature of English glassmaking in the 1840's. Toilet bottles in clear coloured glass were cut with broad vertical facets. Rounded vases and jugs were blown in the semi-translucent 'opaline' metal, painted and gilded with flower designs and classical friezes, or decorated with scenes painted in sepia monochrome or in colours or even transfer printed. Layered glass, in which different colours were superimposed one on top of the other, was frequently cut with mitre-cutting or Gothic patterns, and given an additional painted, gilded, or engraved decoration. In the 1870's and 1880's, when the use of colour was revived, coloured snakes, fish and flowers were applied to vases, and a kind of glass was produced that shaded gradually from one colour to another. There was even glass to imitate carved ivory, glass with a matt 'satin' surface, and a glass with crackled interior and streaks of colour that acquired the name of 'moss agate'.

The globular decanters and hemispherical champagne glasses of the 1840's were well suited to the art of the engraver, and jugs and vases too were engraved with arabesques, Greek designs, hunting-scenes, and designs incorporating birds and flowers. The demand was great enough to attract glass-engravers from the Continent, and two of these, F. E. Kny and William Fritsche went on to use the 'rock crystal' method of engraving in the 1880's, by which lead-glass vases and decanters had their entire surfaces covered with deeply engraved patterns that gave the appearance of carving. At the same time the 'intaglio' technique was being developed by John North-wood, a deep engraved pattern produced with the kind of wheel

PLATE 13 A fine 'Nailsea' jug in green glass flecked with white. Late 18th or early 19th century.

usually employed by the glass-cutter. The Northwoods were also pioneers in other fields, perfecting the technique of etching on glass, which permitted patterns on the most fragile and elegant shapes, and reviving the Roman cameo-glass technique, best displayed in the 'Portland Vase', which was developed on a commercial scale using mainly floral designs.

One of the chief innovators in the Victorian glass industry was Apsley Pellatt (1791–1863), whose main interest was in the revival of ancient techniques and the introduction of foreign styles into England. In 1849 he produced his *Curiosities of Glass Making* in which he discussed many of the Venetian techniques, and in 1851 he displayed his 'ice-glass', which he described as 'Anglo-Venetian'. His 'crystallo-ceramie' or 'cameo incrustation' process, by which cameo portraits were deeply enclosed in cut-glass objects like flasks and paperweights, was filched from the French, and it must be said that through the information he imparted in his book many debased and artless imitations of former styles were produced by his contemporaries.

Of all the glass novelties the Victorians produced, none are more highly sought after than the *millefiori* paperweights, though they are not distinctively different from the paperweights the French had been producing since 1845. An arrangement of tiny coloured glass canes was embedded in clear glass and overlaid with a dome of clear glass that served to magnify the pattern. The English firm of George Bacchus & Son was certainly producing these in 1848, and so was the Islington Glass Works of Rice Harris in 1849.

Table centrepieces became popular in the 1860's, and were variously called 'epergnes', 'flower-stands', 'plateaux', 'fruit and flower glasses', and 'bonbon stands'. Their function was mainly decorative and their design incorporated trumpet-shaped holders, either curved or straight, though the 'flower-stands' also had baskets hung, usually, from close-twisted arms, and the 'plateaux' had mirror bases and were decorated with long, leaf-shaped components.

Ruskin's condemnation of cut-glass had had some influence in certain circles. In 1859, William Morris commissioned the architect

Philip Webb to design some wineglasses and tumblers for him, and these were made at Powell's Whitefriars Glassworks. Powells went on to produce opalescent glass, often in a Venetian style, and made an important contribution to the delicate and slender 'Art Nouveau' style of the end of the century. Another designer, Christopher Dresser, designed some glasses in bubbly, streaky material which were made by James Couper & Sons of Glasgow and called 'Clutha' glasses. Today we can see that these glasses, especially Webb's, marked the beginning of a revival of handmade blown glass, influenced by the restrained designs of Roman and medieval glass, and that they started the tradition for simple and well-designed glass that is the main feature of 20th-century quality glass manufacture.

PLATE 14 Wineglass, the waisted ogee bowl engraved with the words *No Excise* above a barrel. On reverse, a fruiting apple tree. The stem contains an opaque white lace twist and a multi-ply spiral band. Plain foot. The Cider Tax was eventually modified in 1766. 6¼ ins. high. Circa 1763.

2

TECHNIQUES OF
THE GLASSMAKER

Glass in its many forms either colourless, or of water-white clarity, multi-coloured or as opaque as china has always proved to be an article of fascination both to the artist and collector. It is indeed one of the oldest and most beautiful of materials. Its fluidity enables it to be fashioned into an endless variety of shapes, to be cut with scissors, or drawn into threads as fine as silk, and yet it is produced from very commonplace materials.

Fundamentally, the basis of glass is silica, which is freely distributed in the form of sand or combined in clays, granites, and felspars. Sand when mixed with sodium carbonate and fused in the furnace forms a simple glass of pale-green tint commercially known as sodium silicate, which is soluble in water. When lime is added to the sand and soda a stable glass is formed which is insoluble in water. This is known as a soda-lime glass and is used in the manufacture of such everyday articles as electric light bulbs and bottles.

This mix is modified for the making of luxury glasses, imitating natural crystal. In order to produce a crystal glass of water-white clarity more carefully prepared conditions than those used for commercial glass must be observed. Here again the basic component is sand, but of a much purer quality. In this mix the lime and soda are replaced by potash and lead which enhance the transparency and lustre of the glass.

All sands contain impurities and their suitability for the making of crystal glass is determined by their iron content. As little as one part of iron oxide in 5,000 parts of sand is sufficient to impart a sea-green tint to the finished article.

In the 17th and 18th centuries the silica was not obtained from sand but from flint stones. These were burnt and then ground to a fine powder, hence the term 'flint' glass. Single flint or thin flint was a term used to describe vessels made from a single gathering of metal. When a second gathering was added to remedy the tendency for lightness, it was termed double flint.

Early in the 19th century supplies of sand came from Alum Bay in the Isle of Wight, the Lynn river, and Aylesbury. Today, the purest deposits of sand for the best colourless glass are found at Loch Aline in Scotland, at Fontainebleau near Paris, and at New Jersey and Pennsylvania in America.

Potash is added to the batch in preference to soda when the cost of the raw materials is of secondary importance. Potash glass is less prone to discolourisation during melting than glass containing soda as the fluxing agent. This is particularly the case with a glass containing lead. Potash and lead are invariably used in combination for glasses where clearness is essential, such as crystal-glass and the best tableware.

Lead-crystal glass is produced from the fusion of sand, red lead, and potash. As lead is a very heavy substance, it considerably increases the density of the glass, enhancing its power to refract and disperse the light transmitted through it. It is this property of density and ability to disperse light that gives to lead-crystal glass its sparkle and brilliancy when cut, and its bell-like note when sharply struck.

In the early days of lead-crystal glass, borax was added to the mixture solely for its fluxing properties. The most important property of borax when added to a glass mix is its ability to impart to the glass increased resistance against various kinds of shock, such as sharp blows or sudden changes of temperature, and in lead-glasses it prevents cloudiness.

The colour, transparency, and brilliance of a glass mixture are all

PLATE 15 Fireclay pots used for crystal glassmaking. The
smaller 'skittle' pots are used for coloured glass.

enhanced by the presence of a small quantity of arsenic. It is introduced into the glass as white oxide of arsenic in the order of one
part to one thousand parts of sand.

For crystal-glass and good commercial 'white' flint-glass to appear
perfectly colourless when viewed through a thin section, certain
metallic oxides are added to the glass. These oxides are known as
decolourisers. Manganese dioxide, usually in the form of pyrolusite,
is the principal decolouriser for lead-glass. It was undoubtedly used
in the 17th century for decolourising Ravenscroft's glass-of-lead.

Coloured glass has always enlisted admiration and wonder from
the earliest times. The technique of producing coloured glass was
probably first attempted in an endeavour to imitate natural stones.
Colour technology is a complicated science but the Venetians were
obviously able to overcome the problems and to control furnace
conditions.

41

Techniques of the Glassmaker

Many specimens of blue glass were produced by them in the 15th century and green, purple, and opaque white glass were other popular colours. The following are some of the colouring agents used in the manufacture of coloured glasses:

Red	Selenium, copper, and gold
Blue	Iron, copper, and chromium
Yellow	Silver, iron, and cerium
Green	Iron, copper, and chromium
Purple or Violet	Manganese and nickel
White opal	Arsenic, tin, and certain salts

In crystal-glass, small quantities of the colouring agent are either added to the glass mixture itself, or the glass is lightly 'cased' or 'flashed' with a layer of coloured glass when the article is being finished at the furnace. This latter style was very popular in the 19th century. Articles cased in ruby, green, and blue were cut and engraved in various designs to disclose the colourless crystal glass beneath.

The melting of best-quality tableware is conducted in what is described as a pot furnace. The term 'pot' refers to the actual melting crucible housed in the furnace itself.

The preparation of these fireclay pots is an important phase of crystal glassmaking. They are the largest known example of the potter's art, as they are made entirely by hand. They are prepared from special clays selected for their purity, plastic nature, and property of withstanding intense heat.

The process of slowly heating the empty pot to red heat and transferring it to the glass furnace while still hot is probably the most critical period in the life of the pot.

They vary in size according to requirements. In plate 15 are shown the larger pots, three feet six inches high and four feet six inches long, and a smaller kind or 'skittle-pot' usually employed for the coloured glasses.

The making of the best crystal-glass is always conducted in pot furnaces, housing from one to twenty of the fire-clay pots. A model of the type of furnace in general use today is shown in plate 17. It consists of an upper chamber above floor level, containing the pots, and a lower chamber consisting of recuperators. Hot gases from a gas-producer pass through an opening, known as the 'eye' of the furnace, sweep over the pots, escape downwards through ports or openings, to the recuperator tubes, and thence to the stack.

The furnaces used in early times were basically the same as those of modern construction, except that the pots were heated by the direct application of the burning fuel. A model of a glass-melting furnace built to the description of Georgii Agricola of the type used in the 16th century is shown in plate 16. This is a translation of the description of the furnace from *De Re Metallica*, published by Froben at Bâle in 1556:

'The furnace is round, eight feet wide and twelve feet high, strengthened on the outside with ribs, one and a half feet thick, and is composed of three chambers the lowest having a narrow opening for stoking the logs on the ground-level hearth. In the wall of the middle chamber are six arched openings which, when the heated pots are put in, are blocked up with clay, only small openings being left. The thickness of the pot should be two fingers, their height two feet, the breadth of bulge one and a half feet, and of mouth and base, one foot.

'In the centre of the roof of the middle chamber is a square opening, a palm long and broad, through which the heat penetrates into the topmost compartment. At the back of the compartment is an opening, so that in the oblong pottery tunnel placed in it, the glass articles may be cooled off gradually. If they were not thus cooled, they would crack. These tunnels are then taken out of the upper compartment and replaced in their chambers.'

The raw materials required for a glass 'batch' are mixed either by hand or by power-driven machines. Broken glass, or 'cullet' as it is termed, is added to the batch to help in the breaking up of cords and streaks which develop during the melting operation.

In the melting of glass, the mixture of batch and cullet is shovelled into the pot through its mouth until nearly filled, the mouth of the

PLATE 16 Model built to Agricola's description of a 16th-century furnace.

pot is then closed with a fire-clay slab, and the melting commences. After several hours the glass becomes a quiescent, intensely brilliant mass with such a highly reflecting surface that it is difficult to distinguish its level from the gleaming walls of the pot itself.

When the glass responds easily to the glassmaker's demands it is then said to be a 'sweet-natured' metal and is deemed ready for 'working'. The temperature is lowered until the glass attains the correct consistency for the glassmaker to gather and fashion it into the shape he requires.

An article fashioned in the glasshouse is not so much the effort of an individual as that of a team, known in the industry as a 'shop' or a 'chair'. Each member of the team presides over one particular operation in the sequence required to complete the article. The tools employed today can be clearly seen in plate 19 and are very much the same as those used 250 years ago.

In the making of an article such as a wineglass the methods employed by the early glassmaker have changed little with time.

44

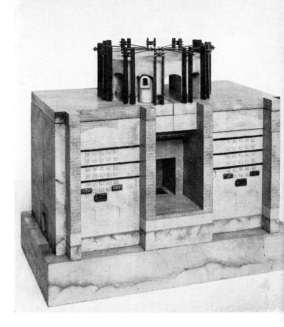

PLATE 17 Model of a modern recuperative gas-fired pot furnace.

Such glasses are made in either a two-piece operation or by the three-piece method, that is, the bowl, the stem, and the foot. In the latter case, the first operation of roughly forming the bowl is carried out by a 'footmaker', the stem is then the task of a 'servitor', and the finishing of the glass is carried out by the 'gaffer', the craftsman in charge of the chair. Usually a few apprentice hands are in attendance to carry away the finished article and generally assist the chair.

The footmaker uses a blow-iron to gather the molten glass from the pot. The blow-iron is an iron pipe, shaped conveniently for blowing by mouth, and at the other extremity thickened into globular form to facilitate the collection of the molten glass. This is shown in plates 18 and 19. He places the end of the blow-iron on the surface of the molten glass and rotates it rapidly with his hands. This causes the glass to adhere to the blow-iron and while still rotating it the footmaker carries it to the 'marver'.

The marver is a flat piece of iron about two or three feet square with a smooth, highly polished surface. Due to the plastic consistency of the molten glass its shape can be altered by a rolling motion across the surface of the marver.

The footmaker occasionally interrupts the marvering operation to blow down his blow-iron to distend the mass of glass into a bulb (plate 18). He may also hold the blow-iron in a vertical position to allow the bulb of glass to extend slowly under its own weight. A typical glasshouse scene is shown in plate 19.

The footmaker has complete control over the plastic mass of glass during the operation of forming the bulb. If he needs to reheat the glass he does this by taking it to a small auxiliary furnace, known as a 'glory-hole'.

After he has completed his task of roughly forming the bulb into the shape of a glass, he now hands it to the servitor who drops a small knob of molten glass upon the end of the bowl. The servitor then reheats it at the 'glory-hole' to make the junction complete. This knob of glass is then drawn out to form the stem leaving a small button of glass at the unattached end. A small amount of molten glass from the pot is gathered on this extremity to form the foot and the servitor then quickly fashions this by flattening it with a pair of wooden 'clappers'.

Now that he has finished his part in the formation of the glass he passes it to the gaffer, who grips the foot by a spring clip attached to an iron rod, termed a 'gadget' in glasshouse parlance.

The gaffer detaches the blow-iron from the bowl of the glass by touching it with a moistened piece of iron and then sharply tapping the blow-iron with it. This causes the bowl to crack completely round its circumference. (See stage 3 in plate 20). He then reheats it and proceeds to remove the surplus glass from the rim of the bowl with a pair of shears. This operation is illustrated in plate 21. The gaffer completes the shape and finishes the edge of the glass with his 'pucellas'. These are also used to adjust the diameter of the bowl. Pucellas or spring tongs are similar to a large pair of sugar tongs.

During the finishing operation the gaffer is seated in his glassmaker's chair. This is a wooden form or long stool. It has attached to it two extended arms along which the gaffer rotates his blow-iron

PLATE 18   Blowing the bowl of a wine-glass.

or gadget with his left hand, while shaping the hot article with his right hand. Upon completion the finished article is then annealed in the annealing furnace to remove any residual stresses.

The annealing furnace or 'lehr' was originally built so that it used waste heat from the working furnace, but today it takes the form of a heated chamber through which passes a continuous conveyor belt.

In the 18th century, before the gadget was invented, the foot of a three-piece wineglass was attached to a 'pontil' for the finishing operation. The pontil is a similar object to the blow-iron, but not quite as thick. When the pontil was used the finished glass was detached from it by a sharp tap, leaving a rough mark on the bottom of the glass. This is known as a pontil mark. It is a characteristic of all 18th-century drinking glasses.

Techniques of the Glassmaker

Applied Decoration on Glass.

The technique of decorating glass by engraving, enamelling, carving, and cutting is by no means a modern innovation. Engraving decorative designs upon glass, for instance, both by the wheel and diamond, have been practised from the earliest times. Specimens of Roman engraving showing shallow cutting executed on a wheel can be seen in the National Museum in Rome and inscribed glasses from the 4th century, engraved by talented artists are extant in the museums of Munich, Vienna, and Venice. Today collectors recognize several types of engraving, including acid-etching and sand-blasting. One of the most prolific and better-known methods is that of wheel-engraving.

Glass engraving by the copper wheel became popular in this country during the 18th century. In 1742 Jerom Johnson, a glass manufacturer, used the term 'flowered glasses' when referring to engraved ware. At that time the most popular motifs were of vine leaves, bunches of grapes, hops and barley, and apple trees. Later, emblematic designs recording a political or social event were depicted. Today those bearing Jacobite emblems are the most popular amongst collectors.

Although the technique of engraving is similar to that of cutting, the process offers much greater scope for artistic expression than cutting. The engraver works with a copper wheel which is rotated in a simple lathe operated by a foot treadle. The wheels, which are interchangeable, vary in size from about four inches in diameter down to the smallest which is not much larger than a pin's head.

The larger wheel is used for simple cutting of facets and grooves and the smaller variety for the intricacies of pictorial and decorative work. The more delicate work requires the use of a finer wheel.

This process requires a great deal of patience and skilful work on the part of the craftsman, and belongs more to the domain of art. Much of the beauty of the work depends on his decision as to the depth of the engraved line. He must also decide which parts of the design are to be left dull and which require polishing. His difficulties are increased by the fact that he has to press the glass against the underside edge of the wheel leaving the part of the surface on which he is working covered by the abrasive medium.

The edge of the wheel is smeared with an abrasive mixture of oil and emery or carborundum powder. The glass is then pressed against the underside edge of the rotating wheel which grinds the desired pattern upon it. The artist is shown engraving a flower motif on a vase in plate 22.

The design is usually marked out on the glass with a mixture of gum and chalk. The engraver then roughs out the main part of the design using a wide wheel with a flat edge and a coarse grain of emery. He then changes the wheel to add the detailed work of the design. When different shading effects are required, wheels of lead, wood, cork, or rubber are employed. For polishing the engraved surface of the finished article, lead or wooden wheels are used. In modern practice, portable high-speed cutting wheels are used for this type of work.

There is plenty of evidence to show that the art of engraving with a diamond point was practised in early Christian times. It was revived by the Venetians in the early part of the 16th century, and later spread to Nuremberg and Antwerp. The art was perfected by such Dutch artists as Anna Roemers Visscher and Willem Jacobsz van Heemskerk, who were able to produce pictures rather than designs on the glass. Their work is marked by its clear transparent nature. The earliest dated English specimen is a Verzelini goblet inscribed 1577.

Diamond engraving can be classified into linear style and stippling. In both cases the same tool is used. It is the sharp point of a diamond or some such hard material, mounted in a suitable holder. The work termed 'diamond-point' engraving is somewhat akin to drawing. When using the tool for linear style engraving, the design is scratched or drawn upon the glass, the shading being accomplished by cross strokes, known as hatch-work. In stipple engraving the design is impressed upon the glass in a series of coalescent dots. They provide the highlights of the design, and the intensity is achieved by varying the closeness of the dots. The shading and background is obtained by leaving the surface more or less alone or by very lightly dotting the blank spaces. Fine lines sometimes appear applied in a very casual manner. They were used to outline a scroll, the end of a sleeve, or as part of a bird's wing. An outstanding artist in this technique is undoubtedly the Dutch artist David Wolff. His style is easily recognised and shows the utmost charm and delicacy.

Cameo engraving or carving in high relief was a very popular art form with the Romans. Specimens are preserved in many museums of Roman glass, both colourless and tinted, showing cameo engraved figure subjects. The Portland Vase, now in the British Museum, London, is without doubt the most perfect and expressive example of cameo engraving. It is of dark-blue glass over which has been superimposed a layer of white opaque glass. Grecian figures have been carved from the outer casing so that they stand out in bold relief against the darker background.

The tools used for this type of engraving are rods of tempered steel varying in size from one-sixteenth to one-eighth of an inch in thickness, held in soft wooden holders much like a pencil, the point of the steel rod being ground to a triangular shape. The body of the specimen to be engraved was 'overlaid' or 'cased' with glass of various colours. The artistry was in removing the unwanted glass so that the design would be left in high relief. Shading is contrived by cutting the outer layer nearer to the dark background, often to the thinness of paper. Good shading added the subtlety of a painting to the sculptural quality of the figure subjects.

For the work on the Portland Vase the surface of the glass was lubricated with paraffin, and the unwanted glass was chiselled away by the sharp edges of the tempered steel tool. Modern artists, however, have the use of hydrofluoric acid to remove the overlay, leaving the figure subjects to be delicately carved by hand. The natural brightness and gloss of the glass is restored by using polishing powders on high-speed lathes.

Glass that has been decorated by having colours painted on it has a great attraction for the experienced collector. Many believe that

PLATE 19 A typical glasshouse scene. The mouth of the pot containing the molten glass is seen on the right with the marver in the foreground.

enamelling on glass displays the greatest artistic achievement of the glass decorator. The Romans were skilled in the art of enamelling, and specimens are extant where they used it with great artistic effect. The technique of enamelling was introduced into this country by artists from Germany and the Low countries. Originally 'thin' or 'wash' enamels were used, but the 'dense' variety eventually became the more popular.

Enamelling on glass can, broadly speaking, be divided into two kinds. That in which the enamel is permanent, where the paintwork is fired on after being applied and that in which the colour is painted upon the surface. In the latter process, after the design has been painted on, it is sometimes varnished in order to render it a little more permanent.

Where the colour is to be permanent, the enamel is made up as a paste consisting of a substance intended to assist fusion, a finely powdered metallic colouring compound, and an oil or water medium to give the paste the required consistency. The artist then applied the paste to the glass using a brush or transfer. When the design is complete the specimen is then fired in a muffle or kiln so that the constituents of the enamel fuse together into a uniform glazed finish.

There are many technical difficulties involved in the making of a satisfactory enamel. In order that the specimen of glass should not be distorted during the firing process, the enamel must obviously fuse at a lower temperature than the softening point of the article itself. It needs to be sufficiently durable to withstand the ravages of time, and the enamel and the glass body must also have corresponding ratios of contraction, or very nearly so.

The technique of decorating glass by removing part of the surface either by an appropriate hand tool or by mechanical means has varied little with time. Hand-operated cutting wheels were in some cases superseded by water power and later, in the 19th century, by steam power. In modern establishments, however, although in some cases certain glass articles are cut by wholly automatic means, the early process of cutting is still used.

The use of the wheel for cutting facets goes back to the very early days of blown glass. The Romans, using as their medium a pure white glass, *cristallum*, were able to cut complicated geometric designs in faceting, the pattern being built up of oval depressions and grooves. They were also adept in the cutting of figure subjects, such as gladiators, cut in shallow outline. Examples of this work can be seen in the National Museum, Rome.

The lead-glass that Ravenscroft perfected lent itself readily to cutting. Annular incisions cut into the glass surface increase the play of light and so enhance the brilliance of the glass itself. The process can be divided into four operations: marking, roughing, smoothing, and polishing. The first step is to mark out on the glass surface the pattern or design to be followed by the cutter. This is usually done with a mixture of red lead and turpentine. In the roughing operation the craftsman follows the pattern marked out by means of a revolving wheel of iron, some 18 inches in diameter. The edge of the wheel can be flat, convex, or V-shaped, depending on the cut required. The cutting edge of the wheel is kept coated with fine, wet sand which streams from a hopper suspended above the wheel. The craftsman presses the vessel firmly against the edge of the revolving wheel and the groove or incision is made by the abrasive action of the wet sand. This roughing operation leaves the glass with a coarse, frost-like finish, very different from the gleaming facets of the finished article.

The roughed outline is then finished on a wheel of sandstone, the edge of which must correspond to the cut already made during the first operation. Additional freehand interlacing cuts necessary to the pattern are added at this stage, usually by similar but smaller stone wheels. The surface of the sandstone is lubricated by a thin trickle of water. Its smooth cutting action quickly removes the rough marks left on the glass surface by the wet abrasive sand.

The smoothing operation is where the skill of the craftsman has full play. For this he needs a steady hand and a keen eye. The design can easily be spoiled if a groove is too long or too deep. The extremities where two cuts meet must exactly coincide, and the surface of the cuts must be smooth and regular.

After the smoothing operation on the sandstone wheel, the incisions and indentations are left with a dull, matt appearance. The original gloss and transparency of the glass are then restored by a polishing operation, using either mechanical or chemical means. The earlier mechanical method required two distinct operations using wooden and felt wheels and fine abrasives, such as putty powder and rouge. The first polish is attained by using a wooden wheel and putty powder, and a final lustre is applied with a cork or felt wheel fed with rouge.

PLATE 20 The process of making a wineglass. (1) The
gathering of glass is blown roughly into the shape of the
bowl of the wineglass. (2) The servitor adds a knob of glass
to the end of the bowl which eventually forms the stem;
more glass is added to form the foot. (3) The gaffer detaches
the blow-iron leaving the rim of the bowl with a jagged edge.
He then shears off the surplus glass to leave a smooth edge.
(4) The finished wineglass.

Techniques of the Glassmaker

In the chemical process, the finished article is dipped for a few seconds into a mixture of hydrofluoric and sulphuric acids. This results in a uniform, highly lustrous surface. Because of the time factor and the excellent finish obtained, the chemical process has almost completely superseded the older method.

The craftsman of the wheel has three basic cuts from which to work. They are the flat (formed with a wheel with a flat edge), the hollow (the wheel used has the edge rounded in a convex manner), and the mitre, for which the wheel is provided with a sharp, V-shaped edge. All cut patterns are made up from these three basic cuts. The designer forms the motifs to make up his pattern and design, in such a manner that they are in harmony and bear some logical relationship, one with another. The usual motifs are: *Hollow hexagons*, cut in hexagonal style, an hexagonal facet being formed at the parts where the curved edges intersect. *The simple hollow*, an oval facet rarely found alone as a motif in the early specimens, also known as a 'punt' and in Ireland as a 'printy' or 'thumb mark'. *Flutes*, either hollowed or sometimes enhanced by notching. These were a common form of decoration on the stems and bowls of 18th century wineglasses. The rounded or pillared flute was a popular style with Irish manufacturers during the early part of the 19th century. *Fans*, and their smaller counterpart, the 'split' or 'sprig'. The fan also forms the basis for the fan escallop or shell border. *The edge flute or slice*, sometimes referred to as a lunar slice. The edge flute forms the basis for the leaf festoons and naturalistic design used by most Irish cutters. *The herring bone*, a series of lightly cut mitres of graduated length, a popular border pattern. This is known to the Irish cutters as a 'blaze'. *The star* was an obvious choice of motif in early cutting. It could be employed alone or as part of a pattern. Its earliest form was six-pointed, but later 18- and 24-pointed stars became the vogue. *Diamonds* in various forms, such as relief, cross-cut, hollow, plain, and strawberry. Undoubtedly, the diamond was the most prolific of all 18th-century motifs. *Alternate panels*, often described as 'hobnail' pattern, used to decorate square spirit decanters. *Prismatic cutting* was a motif introduced by Irish cutters in the late 18th

PLATE 21 The gaffer at work in his glass-maker's chair. He is seen trimming the rim of a bowl with a pair of shears.

century. It usually took the form of horizontal, parallel grooves and was used to decorate the necks of decanters, bowls, and jugs. *Curved motifs* which feature circles and semi-circular figures are the most difficult patterns to cut and are attempted only by the most experienced craftsmen.

It must be appreciated that the quality of the cutting depends entirely on the skill and conscientiousness of the craftsman. He supports the article he is cutting in his hands, and although he may steady his movements by resting his elbows on the bench, no other aid is provided. His work is to a great extent freehand, yet a complicated pattern can be cut with remarkable precision and accuracy.

Although all patterns demand great skill, an indication of good craftsmanship is always to be found in curvilinear designs. Patterns formed on deeply cut curves are the most difficult to execute, the smooth easy flow of the curves indicates an expert craftsman. Still more difficult are curvilinear designs on a curved surface.

An important development in cut-glass technique was the mechanisation in America of the pressing process as applied to glass. The technique of pressing, whereby glass is dropped into a plain

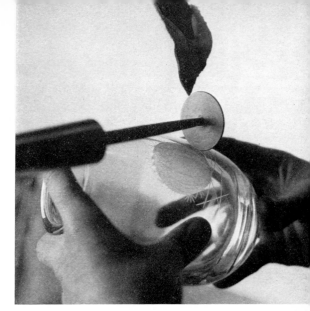

PLATE 22 The engraver at work on a vase. The wheel is lubricated by a thin trickle of oil from the hopper suspended above it.

mould and a plunger descends to press the final shape, was quickly adopted in this country. It required but a short step to carve on the inside of the mould a raised design which would be transferred to the article as a shallow depression while it was being pressed, and by 1851 the technique had developed sufficiently well to allow production of imitations of the cut article.

This principle of mass-production infected the craftsman as much as it impaired his product, and as the pressed article was cheaper to produce than the hand-cut one, the country was soon flooded with pressed glass of this nature. By the middle of the 19th century, the popularity of hand-cut glass had begun to decline. Expensively cut table services and ornamental glass soon lost their appeal when pressed replicas could be bought for so much less.

Another style of applied decoration in the mid-19th century was 'old gold' threaded glass, for which a process was used of closely winding threads of delicately tinted glass over colourless or pale ruby glass. A champagne glass decorated in this manner was shown in a competition held by the Royal Society of Arts in 1869.

'Crystallo-ceramie' was yet another 19th-century innovation.

Techniques of the Glassmaker

This was a process of glass incrustation perfected by Apsley Pellatt, who owned and operated the Falcon Glasshouse in Southwark. It consisted of moulding medallions, portraits, sporting scenes, coats of arms, and floral designs from a porcellaneous material, and enclosing them in the body of vessels, such as paperweights, wineglasses, plaques, and scent bottles. The refractory paste he used to form the incrustations consisted of china clay and a frit of potash and sand.

The use of hydrofluoric acid to etch motifs on the surface of a glass is a comparatively modern technique. Although the process was discovered by Heinrich Schwanhardt of Nuremberg in the 17th century, it was not used to any great extent until the end of the 19th and beginning of the 20th century. For acid embossing, the surface of the glass is completely coated with a compound, such as wax, gum, or varnish. This resist is able to withstand the action of the acid. The design is then drawn through this covering with a fine steel point, allowing the acid to attack the exposed design. After a few minutes treatment, the glass is thoroughly washed and the resist removed.

A variety of finishes can be obtained by modifying the nature of the resist. For instance, a stippled texture can be obtained by sprinkling grains of mica over the glass surface, and by varying the size of the grains, coarse and fine stippling can be achieved. The mica obscures the surface and partially prevents the attack of the acid.

Sandblasting as a means of engraving a design on glass has been adapted to decorative procedures during recent years. Fine grains of sand are directed by high pressure air from a portable 'gun' against the glass surface. The part of the design to be left blank is masked by pasting over the surface a specially treated paper which is impervious to the action of the sand particles. This technique is used today for the decoration of glass panels. In this process a wide range of decorative effects can be obtained by slight modifications, such as altering the size of the nozzle of the gun, and the quality of the sand used. Untold possibilities are available to the creative artist when the two methods, acid engraving and sandblasting, are combined.

3

COLLECTORS AND COLLECTING

Up to a quarter of a century ago the collection of antiques of all kinds was considered to be the prerogative of the wealthy, but nowadays the field is open not only to all those who have a love of old and beautiful things but also to those who wish to save the money they have acquired from being eroded away as sterling decreases in value.

Prior to 1960, antique glass had not received the attention of collectors to the same extent as other fields of collecting, like furniture, paintings, silver, and porcelain. But the rapidly rising prices of the post-war years have driven people to find another outlet for their collective instincts, and glass has been the obvious choice. These enthusiasts include many of the younger generation, perhaps stimulated by the large amount of literature on the subject in book and magazine form that began to appear in the 1950's and is still being produced in response to an almost insatiable demand.

Needless to say, this upsurge of interest brought an inevitable reduction in the quantity of specimens available on the market and prices soared so quickly that many traders discovered, often too late, that their price tickets were outstripped overnight. An article sold for a few pounds might cost them twice as much if they tried to replace it! The tempo has slowed down during the past year, but, in general, 1967 prices are roughly four times those of 1960, and very rare specimens may cost at least six times what they did in

1960. One would have thought that this tendency would bring a diminution in interest, but this is not so. A young and enthusiastic collector remarked, when the point was raised, that 'it is never too late to start collecting antiques', and his statement is reliably supported by the number of satisfied collectors who have jumped on the band-wagon during the last three or four years. This should encourage newcomers and a few hints as to what to look for when examining prospective purchases might be welcome.

Unlike English silver, very little glass produced prior to the 19th century bore marks showing the maker or the date of manufacture. Formation of the specimen is the only guide to its date, and for the details now available to us we are greatly indebted to the many collectors of the late 19th and early 20th centuries who applied themselves wholeheartedly to getting some semblance of order into a subject that had previously been given small thought. One such was A. Hartshorne, whose large treatise, *Old English Glasses* (London, 1897), was the pioneer in this field of literature and still commands respect from later writers, although time and further research have disproved some of the theories advanced.

Therefore, the first thing our student must do is familiarise himself with the various types of glass in what is called the 'Collectors' Period' (1690 to 1830, when the best 'lead' glass was made) by diligent assimilation of the illustrations given in the many text-books that have been published. Many may be found in public libraries, while the rarer volumes are more likely to be seen in the National Museums. Personal acquisition, even if they are available as second-hand copies, may be beyond the finances of the smaller collector. Books figuring the common glasses in addition to those of interest only to the connoisseur will be the most helpful.

The next step is sight and examination of actual specimens, preferably in the stock of a knowledgable trader, who, if he considers you have a receptive mind and are likely to become a future purchaser, will permit you to handle items and be willing to discuss any points you raise. If you are fortunate enough to be the friend of a collector you should examine his collection closely and discuss the merits of the individual pieces with him. Glass of all kinds will be found in the principal museums and many provincial art galleries. Although your knowledge will be increased by a visit to these, specimens are in locked showcases, and glass cannot be fully appreciated when inspected through a glass window. Handling will be of the utmost value in helping you to discriminate between the good and the indifferent, but without special influence or recommendation you are unlikely to be allowed to handle museum pieces.

Next you should begin to familiarise yourself with the points that should be looked for in distinguishing an old glass. After selecting a specimen that has special appeal for you, examine it very carefully and at leisure in good daylight. Eighteenth-century metal, particularly before 1750, has colour tints – greenish, blackish, greyish, or bluish. A steel-blue is especially good. The tints tend to disappear after 1750, and this is especially so in high-quality glasses, but the hard, clear tint of modern crystal will not be seen.

Scrutinise the interior of the bowl for horizontal striations or graining (which can be very pronounced and are never entirely absent) and for faint vertical marks starting a little way below and rising to the bowl rim. The rim should be nicely rounded over, though sometimes a slight irregularity may be felt by passing the fingers around it. This is where the workman withdrew his finishing tool and is not detrimental to the specimen. If a small chip has been removed inexpertly the contour of the rim may be affected and it may feel sharp to the touch. Removal of larger chips can involve a cutting down of the bowl, thereby putting the glass out of proportion. The bowl diameter normally never exceeds that of the foot, and is usually less. Suspect trimming of the foot, if these measurements are reversed.

The stem, presumably, will follow closely that of the text-book illustration, if you have been able to find one. Be wary of any that does not conform with the standard of the period. Quite probably it is not the previously undiscovered specimen that all of us would like to find.

The foot requires the fullest attention, as that is the hardest part of a glass to simulate. A pontil (or punty) mark is certain, but this is a sign of a hand-made vessel and no guide to age; in most cases the foot will be conical (the higher the better), never flat; the edge should be reasonably uniform, for if it is much thicker in one place than elsewhere, trimming out of a chip is probable. A folded foot should be nicely turned under. Although you will find some specimens with most irregular folds, this will not detract from their value unless you are a person that only tolerates perfection. Wear marks will vary (not much may be apparent on a lightweight glass) and ingrained dust is a good sign of antiquity. The bowl too may have wear marks on the rim and will almost always have them inside or outside.

Another essential requirement for collectors of early glass is to acquire the capacity of discerning the difference between 'lead' and 'non-lead' glass. Lightness, colour tints, bubbly metal, and lack of ring when lightly tapped are common characteristics of a glass without lead, but there are non-lead glasses that are heavy enough and have a good enough metal and ring to convince anyone that they are early lead. Then there are others which are quite light and well tinted, are made in bubbly metal, and have barely any ring, which contain lead, and you will not get a ringing response from a lead-metal decanter. Ultimately it all depends on experience; no one can always be correct, but with experience you are more likely to be right than not.

Nineteenth-century glass presents different problems. After 1830 we leave what is generally known as the 'antique' era and arrive in what most collectors of lead-glass treat with disdain, and is termed 'the modern period'. But much glass of these later years is now rightly counted as 'antique' glass, and, coming within the appellation 'Victoriana', now has many adherents. Until recently, information and illustrations were difficult to come by in the field of Victorian glass, but the subject is now taken far more seriously and it is possible to obtain authoritative books on 19th-century glass, Cameo Glass, Victoriana and the like. This is all to the good, for it would be sad if the information were lost and another gap, such as that from Roman times until the 12th century, were left in the history of English glass.

The rummers and Regency types of glass were so popular that their production continued into Victorian times and they are even reproduced today. Later Victorian types can be more easily recognised, sometimes by their mass-produced appearance, often by the clarity and fragility of the crystal. In the mid-Victorian period, classic and ancient forms were copied to serve the taste of the day and to provide variety for a competitive and constantly enlarging market. Hence it is possible to find Venetian-style glasses which may leave one undecided as to whether they are of the 17th or the 19th century, and acknowledged experts in the field have been known to disagree. Only comparison with an authentic 'antique' specimen can reveal the modern glass. It might be said at this point that all glass collectors should acquire some knowledge of the glass output of other countries, especially those from which the glass industry in England is derived (see chapter 1).

The collector of today is in a far more advantageous position than his predecessors. There is plenty of useful literature, and as well as the established dealers (half a century ago there were probably no more than half a dozen) there are the antique shops that have mushroomed throughout the country. Many of them have 'bargains' in profusion, though their prices are generally higher than those of the old, established dealers. Many cities now have an annual Antiques Fair, in which glass has its place, but sad to say it is not unknown for items of doubtful ancestry to appear on these occasions perhaps because the word 'antique' may be applied to anything beyond the ken of the vendor. Up to a few years ago the date 1830 marked the end of the antique period but nowadays many overseas countries will allow duty-free entry for any object over 100 years old, so that in 1967 the first half of the Victorian era is included.

The new collector must try to decide how he is going to build up his collection. Is it going to be done haphazardly by just picking up a piece here and there as fancy dictates? Or is it to be more methodical? It is necessary to decide whether one wants to cover the whole field or to specialise in objects within one group – for instance, air-twists or opaque twists; balusters or Newcastle engraved glasses. Shelf space may confine your activities, for it is no use buying large goblets and bowls, tall candlesticks, *tazze*, decanters, or bottles, if there is nowhere to keep them safely.

The man who decides on a general collection should concentrate on gradually acquiring one specimen from each group, avoiding duplication of bowl, stem and foot forms as much as possible. As knowledge, interest, and available money increase he will probably want to enlarge on one or more parts of his collection and what he has already obtained will channel his interests.

The man who decides to specialise will not find his task any easier. He too will have to try to vary the types of bowls, stems, and feet. If he selects opaque or air-twist stems and endeavours to cover all the many combinations he is unlikely ever to complete his collection.

In recent years a few collectors have turned to the previously despised soda-glass and are finding it an intriguing subject for the inquiring mind. In the past it has been contemptuously dismissed as a competitor to lead-glass, but perhaps in a few years time one of its protagonists may have sufficient data to publish a book on the virtues of this assumedly poor cousin, thus emulating those who did the same for lead-glass nearly three-quarters of a century ago.

You may have read that a slight tap on the bowl of a glass will produce a good ringing sound if it is made of 'lead', but will be quite flat if of 'soda'. This is not always so. Some soda-glasses give quite a vibrant ring, are extremely well made, and are not always easily distinguished from lead specimens. Weight too cannot be taken as a guide. So recourse is made either to the acid test, a smelly business, or more frequently today to an ultra-violet ray-lamp which reveals in no uncertain manner the main constituent – violet-blue for 'lead' and yellow-green for 'soda'.

As your confidence in your ability to spot suitable specimens increases you should begin visiting the numerous auction-rooms where glass is included in the catalogue. Most auction sales are of a general nature but frequently a small consignment of glass will appear. It is only at the London salerooms of Christie's and Sotheby's that a complete sale is devoted to glass, seldom less than bi-monthly during the season, which usually extends from early October to late July. There is open viewing two or three days before the sale and any specimen can be handled and minutely inspected apart from those expected to sell for a very high sum. The object that catches your eye as a possible purchase should be subjected to the routine you have previously found most successful. Unfortunately the object you want may be in one lot with others, and you will have to take the whole lot, if giving a successful bid, and dispose of the surplus items to the best advantage, probably to a dealer. You may need help in assessing a likely purchase price for the lot. The auction-room office will give an estimated figure, but this will be given to all inquirers and if the lot is of especial interest it is probable that the bidding prices will exceed their valuation. It is best to decide beforehand what it is worth to you, and to mark your catalogue clearly with a maximum figure which, despite the excitement of the moment when the lot comes up for bidding, you must refuse to overshoot. Should the lot fall to you, you will have to wait until the end of the sale before you can approach the auctioneer's clerk, pay the amount due, and take possession of the purchase. If you are wise you will arrive at the auction-room at least half an hour before the beginning of the sale in order to take a final look at the piece you want to ensure that it has not been damaged since you last inspected it. Such incidents do occur and unless the auctioneer is extremely sympathetic you are unlikely to obtain redress, it being a condition of purchase that the bidder is fully aware of all defects in his purchase, though they may not be mentioned in the description in the catalogue.

Finally, the observations of R. S. Williams-Thomas on the 'bloom' or opaque dullness found on some old glasses may be of use to collectors. There are two types of 'bloom', the first caused by lack of durability, the second being called 'sulphur bloom'. In the former the deficiency may take the form of an overall surface film, which can be easily wiped away in its early stages but which gradually becomes a permanent feature of the specimen and may result in the surface of the glass becoming crizzled all over with tiny cracks. The defect can affect glasses of lead, lime, soda, or silica composition, and is due to an unstable batch composition of the glass in which there is too large a proportion of alkali. The excess alkali is leeched away into the atmosphere, leaving only the more stable constituents, with the surface pitted and white. But glass of a fairly good quality can also be affected if, over a period of years, it is attacked by dust, or scratched by continual cleaning with an abrasive material, or has its natural polish affected by acid liquors.

'Sulphur bloom' is only found on glasses which have been reheated at a furnace for the purpose of shaping or shearing. This process may either result in an all-over film or cause a distinct band round the specimen at such a distance from the top as to show that the attack has taken place where the heat of the fire is less intense. Though the leadless glasses are the most susceptible, any glass, when exposed to a sulphur-containing flame under furnace conditions insufficiently heated to consume the sulphur, are liable to be marked, the sulphur in the flame combining with the glass constituents to form a chemical change of an opaque nature on the surface of the glass. But it is necessary to be careful in one's diagnosis, for the remains or fixative of some former gilding or enamelling that has been worn away may have a similar appearance. 'A simple test for sulphur bloom is to wet the fingers and moisten the affected surface. The glass will then be bright in the streak, but the film will quickly reappear as the moisture dries, coming inwards from the edges of the moistened patch. The difficulty of recognising the remains of gilding fixatives may be overcome by remembering that in these cases the marking should show either a faint metallic sheen or the semblance of the original outline of a pattern as its epitaph or ghost.'

Glass can also be discoloured or stained by certain liquids, especially lime in water which leaves a deposit like a permanent stain. This particular discolouration can be removed by soaking in distilled water, careful rubbing, and the use of detergent.

4

FAKES AND FORGERIES

As is to be expected, antique glass has received the attentions of the nefarious, though not to the same extent as silver, paintings, furniture, and other works of art where the perpetrator, if undetected, is likely to be rewarded in greater measure for his labours.

Forgery may be defined as the making of a glass in the style of an earlier century, or the altering or decorating of a period glass to give it greater importance than it would normally have, with full intention to sell it and to deceive the purchaser. In this sector only expensive balusters and engraved glasses such as Jacobites and Williamites could, one would imagine, bring sufficient financial benefit to the forger. The objects would have to be produced and placed on the market singly, for the sudden appearance of a number of rarities on the market, with no certain history or record of earlier ownership, would assuredly arouse suspicion. During the past few years some forgeries have made their appearance but experts soon discovered the deception. Newly-made specimens are more easily recognized as the texture of the metal is too clear or pure, too white and brilliant.

When a genuine period glass, previously unengraved, is decorated with designs or inscriptions, it is more difficult to detect. However, the copying of anything by hand is a tricky business, and mistakes in the pattern or differences in technique as well as lack of information about the history of the glass are soon pounced upon by the knowledgeable.

A prominent glass-maker during the early part of the 20th century, H. J. Powell of the firm of James Powell & Sons, stated that a glass can be so scientifically faked in workmanship, weight, colour, feel, ring, and signs of wear, all of which can be imitated, that discovery is exceedingly difficult, and that we can only be sure about those specimens with an accurate, written history. Unfortunately most antiques were not supplied with 'birth certificates' at the time of making, hence the purchaser must rely upon his own instinct or trust the person from whom the article is acquired. In the latter case a guarantee of authenticity should be obtained providing for return of the specimen and refund of price paid if subsequent investigation reveals a doubtful provenance. Most reputable firms already do this, for they are quite aware that professed experts are not always right, and that the forger or faker is learning from past errors. Modern science and chemistry have discovered many previously unknown facts about the composition of period glass, for which anyone with the ability and inclination to produce fake specimens must be grateful. Their talents could be better applied to advancing modern design and techniques, no doubt to greater financial advantage and prestige, but in many the 'lone wolf' characteristic is inherent and pleasure is derived from fooling the public, monetary gain being of smaller importance.

What are the points one must look for in an effort to differentiate between the 'wheat' and the 'chaff'?

With engraved glasses, comparison of the design and inscription with that on an authenticated glass may show slight imperfections or crude workmanship in the copying of the design or wording, or it may show up whiter than an 18th century engraving.

On most glasses made before 1800 the pontil mark (a jagged finish at the base of the stem) is normal, although of course it is copied in modern reproductions. Some facet-stem glasses of the 1780 period and others after about 1800 had the pontil mark ground off or polished out. Because of this jagged pontil, which in some instances will be found to be as much as a quarter-inch long, a conical or domed foot was necessary to allow the glass to stand firm. In later years, as the foot became flatter, it was necessary to polish out the pontil and today when the feet are completely flat you will find little evidence of any pontil mark.

A fake is something that is not in its original condition, a broken part having been replaced with a piece of more modern manufacture, disguised so as to be passed off as the genuine complete article. In the field of glass this can be effected by providing new bowls, stems or feet for drinking vessels, although the surviving part would have to be of value to make the procedure worth while. Of course, it is not always possible to draw a distinction between a malicious fake and a genuine repair. Chandeliers in particular have to be restored with new arms or branches, candle-pans and drops, if period replacements from discarded chandeliers cannot be found. Wine-glasses too, where the surviving part is of sufficient merit to warrant the expense, can be repaired by affixing a bowl, stem, or foot from a 'written-off' vessel of the same period. With the skill of the repairer and the adhesives available today it is almost impossible to detect where and which part has been replaced.

In another category comes the reproduction of interesting and marketable items, produced by manufacturers whose concern was to supply a public demand using less valuable materials than might be expected. Because a glass is made from 'soda' instead of 'lead' it does not follow that it is a fake. It may be of the right period, but made for a cheaper outlet, unless it was the maker's intention to deceive the public, and who can say it was?

Many early types of glass have been repeated in later years. Cameo glass, for instance, was developed again in the second half of the 19th century following the pattern of the world-famous 'Portland Vase', and there are records of extreme rarities, such as a Verzelini goblet, and the Royal Oak goblet, being copied. Other reproductions include Jacobite 'Amen' and 'Portrait' glasses, air-, opaque and colour-twists, Williamites, and paperweights; but seldom can they bear comparison with a known genuine specimen. If an unwitting

Fakes and Forgeries

collector should become saddled with one of these objects he must put it down to 'buying his experience'. Perhaps, in the long run, it may have been money well spent, saving him from more drastic pit-falls.

E. B. Haynes says some convincing 'Amen' forgeries were put into circulation during the 1930's. It is not improbable that some of these are still lurking amidst private collections with their owners happily believing in their authenticity, and minute examination is vital if and when more 'Amen' glasses reappear on the market, either privately or through a saleroom.

There is the possibility that one or more of an excellent set of glasses may have been irretrievably damaged. What would be more natural than that the owner, unable to find a contemporary replacement, had others specially made to fill the gap? If this had happened 150 or 200 years ago, who today could pinpoint the replacements? It might be more noticeable if effected later in the 19th century when glassmaking became more commercialised, tending towards less individuality in production.

Inferior-quality glasses in the opaque and colour-twist categories usually employ a much thinner enamel, the colours are very different in hue from those of a better glass, and the twists themselves are usually poor. This latter comment applies also to air-twists. But, as previously stated, these may not have been produced primarily as fakes but merely as copies of outstanding specimens for purchase by the less wealthy during the period of their popularity. How was the manufacturer to known that in the mid-20th century single pieces were likely to change hands for pounds or tens of pounds instead of for the shillings he probably charged?

5

MUSEUMS AND COLLECTIONS

Many of the national and provincial museums or art galleries contain a collection of glass from all countries, formed either by bequest or purchase on the open market, and most of this is available for public inspection. Some have a surfeit of specimens, which have to be held in storage owing to lack of display facilities, and those with sufficient influence to gain access 'behind the scenes' would be astonished at the volume and sight of some objects seldom put on view.

Bequests, particularly those comprising items of little rarity, which are already represented in the museum collection, can be an embarrassment, especially if accompanied by the proviso that no specimens should be disposed of. No doubt many museum authorities would prefer to use their own discretion in deciding whether the objects should be retained, or sold so that the funds realised could be put to better use in acquiring specimens that would fill gaps in the historical sequence of their collections. In these days, with a number of affluent private collectors anxious to gain possession of desirable specimens, museums, and other public or municipal authorities, working on a limited annual budget, are unable to compete on the open market to the extent they would like. On the other hand, private ownership has its advantages. There is always the likelihood of a collection coming again into the saleroom owing to the pressure of death duties or the heavy incidence of taxation, thus giving another generation the opportunity to acquire and enjoy the art of collecting. Also, some collectors only retain specimens for a few years, during which they accumulate all the facts previously published about them, adding any further information where they can, and when this has been done they sell the piece and reinvest the money realised in other glasses to which they can give similar study.

Museums, over the years, have added considerably to the knowledge of glass history. Through analysis of the specimens that pass through their hands, many authoritative works and reference books have been produced by officials employed in such institutions. For this reason, archaeologists who find what they presume to be some old glass, whether intact or broken, during their excavations should first offer it to one of these bodies so that it can be carefully examined and the information used to assist research into the subject. Broken pieces are of immense help as analysis can be undertaken without the remorse that would be caused by the breaking down of a complete object.

Of later years some of our premier glass manufacturers have created their private museums and libraries to stimulate interest and ideas for their designers and other employees, some of whom have now become devoted collectors themselves. One of the foremost companies in this field are Messrs. Pilkington Bros. of St. Helens, who, in the brief period since 1962, have built up an excellent collection under the guidance of one of our leading dealers. Another of longer standing is the Stourbridge Borough Collection comprising in the main 19th-century glass, to which the local manufacturers and inhabitants have generously contributed.

There are, without doubt, private collections in the British Isles that can compare with, or even excel, those displayed in public museums and art galleries. Very few have had catalogues produced, and where it has been done issue has been limited. To foster better relations among collectors and to increase their knowledge, the Circle of Glass Collectors was formed in 1937, and received sufficient support to enable a Commemorative Exhibition of nearly 400 specimens, loaned by more than sixty members, to be staged in the

Museums and Collections

Victoria and Albert Museum from May to July 1962. Joining the Circle confers many privileges on members. Meetings are held periodically, usually in the home of one of the collectors, thus giving everyone the opportunity to see items they may not themselves possess in an atmosphere where the merits and demerits of this enthralling hobby are the principal topic for discussion. Occasionally further interest is stimulated by the reading of a paper covering an aspect of the subject, written specially for the occasion. Those readers desirous of more details should write to the Secretary. Dealers are not permitted to be members.

Overseas, some of the best English glass of all periods is housed in museums and private collections in the United States. As a younger country it has had to develop its artistic collections in a relatively short space of time. That it has done so to the extent of breasting the rest of the world is of great credit to the pioneers and to their subsequent education of a mixed European population who doubtless brought to bear the knowledge acquired in their own country. There is little indication of a successful glass industry in the United States prior to the 18th century, and progress at first was slow. Only the development of a mechanical means of production from the invention of press moulding in the United States in the early 19th century made American glass production into a large and prosperous industry.

Hence, in order to build up a collection showing the evolution of glass from earliest times, specimens have had to be acquired from abroad. This has been done with tremendous thoroughness, as is revealed by the amount of glass now on public view in American museums and art galleries and in such private collections as have been seen by visitors from England. The specimens have been selected with great discernment and, so far as private collections are concerned, the adjective used by one accustomed to seeing only the best was 'staggering'.

Acquisition from England during the past quarter of a century has been made easier by the rate of exchange, much in favour of the dollar, and through a special tax concession to American purchasers of antiques from abroad, which gives them great advantages over their English competitors. This has prevented the retention of many desirable glasses in the United Kingdom but the earning of dollars carries such weight with the Chancellors of our Exchequer that there has been no mention of granting similar inducements to the British buyer.

Principal glass collections:

ABERDEEN: Art Gallery and Industrial Museum.
            European glass.

BARNARD CASTLE: The Bowes Museum.
            A small quantity of good glass.

BATH: Victoria Art Gallery.
            Early English and 19th-century Venetian glass.

BEDFORD: Higgins Museum.
            Formed by the late Mr. Cecil Higgins, this collection of English and European glass is considered to be one of the finest in England.

BIRMINGHAM: City Museum and Art Gallery.
            Numerous cartoons for stained glass. Some admirable examples of Roman glass, also Murano and Venetian glass, and lead-crystal.

BOURNEMOUTH: Russell-Cotes Art Gallery and Museum.
            Lead crystal and other glass.

BRADFORD: Bolling Hall Museum.
            Lead crystal and other glass, especially of Yorkshire manufacture. Also bottles.

BRIERLEY HILL, STAFFS.:   Public Library.
            The Stourbridge Borough Collection of Victorian glass.

BRISTOL: City Museum and Art Gallery.
            Local coloured glass of the 18th and 19th centuries, and lead crystal.

Museums and Collections

BURY ST. EDMUNDS: Moyse's Hall Museum.
Early glass of local interest and some 18th-century glass.

BUXTON: Public Library and Museum.
Lead crystal and coloured glass.

CAMBRIDGE: Fitzwilliam Museum.
The well-known Beves collection.

CANTERBURY: Royal Museum and Public Library.
Good examples from Roman and Anglo-Saxon sites. English medieval glass and fragments.

CARDIFF: National Museum of Wales.
Some 18th-century bottles, silver-mounted lead crystal and fragments from Welsh Roman-British sites.

EDINBURGH: Royal Scottish Museum.
English, Venetian, Persian, Arabian, Greek, Roman, and Chinese glass.

EXETER: Royal Albert Memorial Museum.
The Henry Hamilton Clarke Collection of English glass.
Historical Museum.
17th- and 18th-century bottles.

FARNHAM, DORSET: Pitt Rivers Museum.
Good collection of ancient glass from the Near East.

GLASGOW: Art Gallery and Museum, Kelvingrove.
Good collections of Syrian, Venetian, and Spanish glass; some German glass and stained glass; loan collection of lead crystal.

GLOUCESTER: Folk Museum, Bishop Hooper's Lodging.
English glass.

IPSWICH: Christchurch Mansion.
The Tibbenham Collection of Old English drinking glasses; small but good collection of medieval and other fragments.

Museums and Collections

LIVERPOOL: Public Museums.
Good collection of ancient glass, examples of post-Renaissance European glass including Bristol, façon de Venise, and German.

LONDON: Bethnal Green Museum.
Venetian 19th-century glass.
British Museum.
One of the leading general collections in the country.
Guildhall Museum.
Fine collection of ancient glass from London sites, 15th- to 18th-century bottles and phials, and lead-crystal.
Jewish Museum.
London Museum.
The Garton Collection of lead crystal, one of the finest assembled privately; bottles of the 17th century and earlier; some ancient glass.
Science Museum.
Scale models of ancient glasshouses; process exhibits; Wealden fragments (Winbolt Collection).
Victoria and Albert Museum.
A wonderful collection of glass from ancient to modern times.

MANCHESTER: City Art Gallery.
Lead crystal and some good examples of 18th-century South Lancashire glass.
University Museum.
Egyptian and Syrian glass; Alexandrian cut crystal.

NEWCASTLE-UPON-TYNE: Laing (Municipal) Art Gallery and Museum.
Good collection of North country, Newcastle and Gateshead 18th- and 19th-century glass; some lead

Museums and Collections

crystal; 16th- to 18th-century phials from London sites.

NEWPORT, MONMOUTHSHIRE: Corporation Museum and Art Gallery.
Lead crystal; German; 19th-century glass (mostly coloured); ancient fragments from local sites.

NORWICH: Castle Museum.
Flint glass; some Absolon pieces; glass from Roman sites.

OLDHAM: Municipal Art Gallery.
Part of the Francis Buckley Collection of old glass, mainly of North Country origin.

OXFORD: Ashmolean Museum.
Very good Syrian glass; good English bottles; some other glass.

SHEFFIELD: City Museum, Weston Park.
Syrian glass, 16th- to 17th-century German glass, English lead-crystal and other glass mostly of Yorkshire manufacture.

TRURO, CORNWALL: County Museum and Art Gallery.
Lead-crystal and other glass.

For collectors who travel to Ireland or the United States, the following are the principal collections:

IRELAND BELFAST: Ulster Museum, Stranmillis.
DUBLIN: National Museum.

U.S.A. CORNING, N.Y.: The Corning Museum of Glass.
NEW YORK: Metropolitan Museum of Art.
PHILADELPHIA, PA: Museum of Art.
TOLEDO, OHIO: Museum of Art.
WILLIAMSBURG, VIRGINIA: Colonial Williamsburg.

6

CHRONOLOGY FOR COLLECTORS

c. 1226. Laurence Vitrearius settles at Dyer's Cross, near Chiddingfold.

c. 1240. He is making window-glass for the abbey of Westminster.

1300. His son, William le Verrir, has succeeded him, and Chiddingfold receives a Royal Charter.

c. 1350. The Schurterre family has captured the Wealden glass industry.

1435. The Peytowe family is competing.

c. 1549. Carré arrives from Antwerp, erects a furnace in London and others in Surrey; he establishes modern glassmaking in England.

1567. He secures a licence, and (1572) dies.

1575. Jacopo Verzelini is granted the sole right to make Venice glasses in England for 21 years (December 15); his Crutched Friars glasshouse is destroyed by fire.

1588. An inventory is made of the Earl of Leicester's glass at Kenilworth Castle.

1592. Verzelini retires from business; Sir Jerome Bowes takes over, secures a more exclusive licence for 12 years, at an annual rent.

1594. (August) James VI gives a banquet at Stirling Castle

to celebrate the baptism of his son; much 'crystal-line glass gilt with gold and azure' is used.

1611. Coal-burning furnaces are in use; a comprehensive patent is issued to Sir Edward Zouche and partners.

1615. An Edict, prohibiting the use of timber as fuel, is issued.

1614/15. (January) Sir Robert Mansell joins the Zouche board, and by

1623 he has bought out his partners and assumed sole control of glassmaking in England and Wales.

1621. The Tyne ships coal to Mansell's Broad Street furnace.

1627. Mansell buys out the Fifeshire glassmakers.

1637. The Glass Sellers' Company protests at the alleged poor quality of Mansell's glass.

c. 1650. Mansell's monopoly dissolves, and (1656) he dies.

1660–74. George Villiers, second Duke of Buckingham, usurps Mansell's position.

1662. Dr. Merret translates Neri's *Art of Glass* into English.

1662. Charles II marries Catherine of Braganza, and the 'Royal Oak' goblet is made.

1664. A Charter is granted to the Glass Sellers' Company.

1667–73. John Greene corresponds and trades with Allesio Morelli of Murano.

1673. Backed by the Glass Sellers' Company, George Ravenscroft builds the Savoy glasshouse, and in

1674 he receives a patent to make glass (May).

1675. Da Costa is working for Ravenscroft at Henley-on-Thames.

1676. (June) Ravenscroft has introduced lead into his metal: The Company announces that faults have been remedied; a plain seal is (? now) introduced to mark the 'perfect' glasses.

1677. (May) The 'raven's head' seal is adopted and Ravens-croft executes a new three-year Agreement with the Company.

Chronology for Collectors

1677/8. Ravenscroft determines his Agreement, and (May, 1861) dies.

1682. (February) Hawley Bishopp officially takes over the Savoy glasshouse.

1682. (May) The new lead metal ('flint') glasses are in production.

1685. Death of Charles II; accession of James II; commencement of the 'baluster stem' period.

1688. (June 10) Birth of James Frances Edward Stuart.

1688. (November 5) William of Orange lands, by invitation, at Torbay: James II is deported to France (December 23).

1689. William becomes William III of England and reigns jointly with his wife, Mary.

1690. Battle of the Boyne.

1694. Death of Queen Mary.

1702. Death of William III: Queen Anne succeeds.

1707. Union of England and Scotland.

1710. Foundation of the Jacobite 'Cycle Club'.

1713. Peace of Utrecht, terminating the War of the Spanish Succession.

1714. Death of Queen Anne: George I ascends the throne; period of 'moulded pedestal stemmed glasses' begins.

1715. Jacobite rebellion.

1720. (December 20. O.S.) Prince Charles Edward Stuart is born.

1725. (February 23. O.S.) Prince Henry Benedict Stuart is born.

1725. Period of 'baluster stems' is closing; period of 'balustroid stems' is opening.

1727. Death of George I: George II ascends the throne.

1735. Period of 'light (Newcastle) baluster stems' is opening.

1740. Period of 'plain straight stems' is opening.

1741.   (? 1745) Prince Charles Edward is represented on Jacobite rose glasses by an additional bud.

1745.   Battle of Fontenoy; final Jacobite rebellion, and battle of Culloden Moor (1746); Prince Charles escapes to France.

1745/6.   An Excise Act levies a tax on the contents of the glass-pot.

1747.   The Dunvegan Castle 'Amen' glass is engraved.

1748.   Peace of Aix-la-Chapelle, ending the War of the Austrian Succession.

1749.   The Drummond Castle and Mesham 'Amen' glasses are engraved.

1750.   Portrait glasses of Prince Charles Edward begin to appear, including a few in enamel colour by an unknown artist.

1750.   Period of the 'interior twist' glasses is opening.

1756–63.   The Seven Years War, concluding with the Treaty of Paris; particularly marked by Privateer, King of Prussia, and Britannia glasses.

1760.   Period of the 'faceted stem' glasses is opening.

1760.   Death of George II: George III ascends the throne.

1762.   A Prince of Wales is born; Beilby decorates armorial goblets in enamel colours to mark the occasion.

1765.   Period of the 'moulded pedestal stem' glasses and the 'balustroid' glasses is ending.

1766.   Death of James Francis Edward; mourning glasses are made for loyal Jacobites; rose glasses revert to the single-budded pattern.

c. 1762–87.   Michael Edkins paints and gilds Bristol glasses.

1770.   Opaque white Bristol glass is being made.

1775.   Period of 'plain straight stemmed' glasses is ending; period of 'short or rudimentary stem' glasses is beginning.

1775–83.   War of American Independence, ending with the Peace of Paris.

Chronology for Collectors

1777. A new Excise Act doubles the duties, but does not apply to Ireland.

1780. Ireland granted free trade; English glassmakers set up in Ireland and prosper; period of the 'light (Newcastle) baluster stem' glasses and the 'interior twist' glasses is ending.

1793–1801. War of the French Revolution, concluding with the Treaty of Amiens (1802).

1801. Union of Ireland with England and Scotland.

1803–15. Napoleonic Wars, terminating with the Second Treaty of Paris.

1810. Period of the 'faceted stem' glasses is ending.

1820. Death of George III: George IV ascends the throne.

1821. Apsley Pellatt takes out a patent for 'crystallo-ceramie'.

1825. Irish-made glass is first taxed.

1830. George IV dies: William IV ascends the throne.

1837. William IV dies: Queen Victoria ascends the throne.

1845. Excise Acts repealed; the first dated paperweights are made in France.

1850. Period of the 'short or rudimentary stemmed' glasses is ending.

1851. The Great Exhibition.

1859. William Morris commissions Philip Webb to design wineglasses and tumblers for him.

7

GLOSSARY

Ale glass:	Long, but fairly narrow bowl, sometimes waisted, with a capacity of 3 to 4 ozs; the rim diameter usually about $2\frac{1}{4}$ inches. The ale of the 18th century was far more potent than it is today and taken in smaller quantity.
Short ale:	As before, but with a shorter stem.
Dwarf ale:	As before, but stem very short, may comprise only one or two knops, or be stemless.
Giant ale:	More than 12 inches high, with greater capacity.
Armorials:	Heraldic insignia or other devices, often found engraved on some of the best English and Continental glasses.
Baluster:	Curved form, slender above and bulging out below, called a 'true baluster'. When used upside down, designated an 'inverted baluster'.
Beaker:	A forerunner of the tumbler, found with or without a foot rim. Capacity varies.
Cartouche:	An ornament, originally a scroll of paper, adapted for use by engravers to enclose coats of arms or other designs.

Glossary

Caudle:	A hot spiced drink made of oatmeal gruel flavoured with wine or ale, sugar, and spice, dating from the 17th century. Dispensed from a two-handled and spouted cup, not unlike a teapot, especially when fitted with a cover as some were. (See Posset.)
Champagne:	The bowl diameter is equal to or greater than its depth. Capacity 6 ozs.
Low champagne:	As before, but with a shorter stem and capacity 4 ozs.
Cordial:	Small bowl on a tall, rather thick, stem; capacity 1 oz.
Short cordial:	As before, but stem of normal length; capacity 1 to $1\frac{1}{2}$ ozs.
Semi-cordial:	As before but stem of normal length and thickness.
Dram:	Bowls vary in size, stems as dwarf ale above; capacity up to 3 ozs.
Festoon:	Garland of fruit, flowers, or foliage hanging in a curve.
Finial:	An ornament surmounting a cover.
Fluting:	Channelled decoration, vertical, oblique or curved. Moulded flutes are found on some ancient glass but do not appear on English glass until the mid-18th century.
Gadrooning:	A lobed border of convex curves frequently found on the bowl and base of early lead-glass (late 17th and early 18th centuries) and continued much later.
Goblet:	The bowl large in comparison with height of stem; capacity 4 ozs or more.
Giant goblet:	Over 10 inches high.
Mammoth goblet:	Over 12 inches high.
Knop:	A boss or knob on the stem of a glass, candlestick, etc., or used as a finial on a cover.

Glossary

Mug:	Tumbler with a handle.
Porringer:	A two-handled bowl, with or without a cover.
Posset glass:	Of jelly-glass style with a pair of handles and a spout; capacity 2 to 3 ozs.
Posset pot:	A low cylindrical vessel with a pair of handles and a spout, and originally a cover; capacity up to 15 ozs. Posset was made from hot milk curdled with ale or wine, sweetened and spiced, served at country weddings up to the mid-18th century. (See caudle.)
Ratafia:	A cordial flavoured with kernels of almonds, peaches, or cherries, which found favour towards the end of the 17th century. The glass of this name has a very narrow tapering funnel bowl with a stem of approximately the same length, and bowl diameter rarely exceeds $1\frac{3}{4}$ inches; capacity 1 to $1\frac{1}{2}$ ozs.
Reeding:	A decoration consisting of narrow, parallel, convex ridges.
Rummer:	Goblet with a short stem. Not before 1770. Capacity 4 ozs. or more.
Tankard:	A footed mug.
Toasting glass:	Small goblet or wineglass on an exceptionally thin stem; capacity 2 to 4 ozs.
Toastmaster glass:	Cordial or dram with a highly deceptive bowl; capacity $\frac{1}{2}$ to $\frac{3}{4}$ oz.
Tumbler:	A vessel with slightly sloping sides on a flat base.
Wine:	Capacity 2 to 3 ozs.

8

BIBLIOGRAPHY

Percy Bate, *English Table Glass*. (London, 1913)

Geoffrey W. Beard, *Nineteenth Century Cameo Glass*. (Newport, 1956)

J. Bles, *Rare English Glasses of the Seventeenth and Eighteenth Centuries*. (London, 1926)

Francis Buckley, *History of Old English Glass*. (London, 1925)

Arthur Churchill Ltd., *History in Glass*. (London, 1937)

Derek Davis, *English and Irish Glass*. (London, 1965)

E. M. Elville, *The Collector's Dictionary of Glass*. (London, 1961)
    English Tableglass. (London, 1951)
    English and Irish Cut Glass, 1750–1960. (London, 1953)
    Paperweights and other Glass Curiosities. (London, 1954)

J. Arnold Fleming, *Scottish and Jacobite Glass*. (Glasgow, 1938)

Grant R. Francis, *Old English Drinking Glasses*. (London, 1926)

D. R. Guttery, *From Broad Glass to Cut Crystal*. (London, 1956)

Albert Hartshorne, *Old English Glasses*. (London and New York, 1897)

E. Barrington Haynes, *Glass Through the Ages*. (London, 1959)

W. B. Honey, *English Glass*. (London, 1946)

G. Bernard Hughes, *English, Scottish and Irish Table Glass*. (London, 1956)

H. J. Powell, *Glassmaking in England*. (Cambridge, 1923)

S. Ruggles-Brise, *Sealed Bottles*. (London and New York, 1949)

Bibliography

W. A. Thorpe, *A History of English and Irish Glass*, 2 vols. (London, 1929)
    English Glass. (London, 1935)
Hugh Wakefield, *Nineteenth Century British Glass.* (London, 1961)
M. S. Dudley Westropp, *Irish Glass.* (London, 1920)

Periodicals

Antiques (New York)
Antique Collector
Antique Dealer and Collector's Guide
Apollo
The Connoisseur
Country Life
Arthur Churchill Ltd., *Glass Notes.* (From 1946 to 1956)

PART II

A
Sequence
of
Photographs

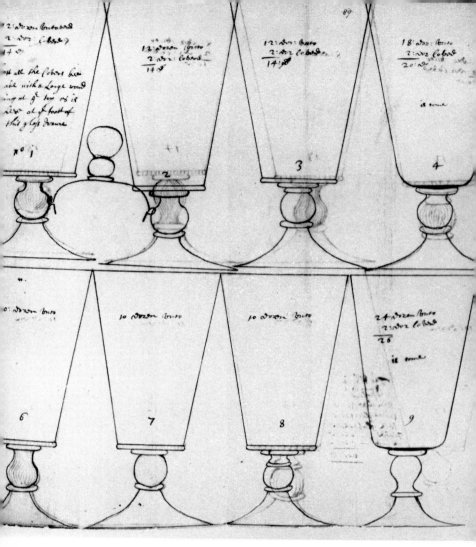

PLATE 23   One of a series of drawings sent to Venice about
1670 by John Greene, member of the Glass Sellers' Company, when ordering glass for the English market. An endeavour to break away from the traditional Venetian style
will be noted. The metal envisaged was probably thicker than
that previously used. The V-shaped bowl was developing
towards the bucket and round funnel shapes. The short
knopped stems show the squat beginnings of the true inverted
balusters.

SEVENTEENTH CENTURY
GLASS

The period from the prohibition of the use of wood fuel in 1615 to the institution of the first tax on English glass by William III's government (War Tax 1695 to 1699) was one in which England was part of a European glassmaking industry, its skilled labour force being international. Hence English design followed that of the Continent and it is difficult to distinguish between English and European productions.

Medical glassware in green glass had been known since the 14th century. Small containers for toilet preparations and perfumes for the use of apothecaries were called *violls* (phials) in Mansell's time. They were mostly in a medieval style, marking an important stage in the development from the containers of Roman days to the modern cylindrical medicine bottles in white glass. Green glass bottles may have been made in the 16th century, but it was not until late in the 17th century that the production of wine bottles became really lucrative. Initially they had bulbous or dome-shaped bodies, and necks of about the same height as the bodies, and were made in thin, fragile glass. Later a thicker metal was used, the bodies were rounder, the necks at first longer, then gradually shortening as the century progressed. Many examples bear seals with arms, initials or other devices to the order of the person for whom the bottle was made.

Apart from these bottles there is very little other glass of the pre-Ravenscroft era available for collectors. What remains of the Bowes, Mansell, and Buckingham glass has gone into museums, except for a very few pieces of Buckingham glass that form part of some private collections.

PLATE 24   Three dwarf ale glasses. The quality of the lead ▲
metal and the heavy gadrooning shows them to be late 17th
century. *Left*: Conical bowl set directly on a domed foot.
Centre: Round funnel bowl on a wrythen annular and a half
knop. *Right*: Round funnel bowl on a wrythen knop and a
half knop.

►PLATE 25   Brownish-tinted metal is familiar in early soda
glasses and also English soda and lead glasses. These two
soda specimens are of that tone in very thin metal, the bowls
with moulded flutes rising into four rows of honeycombing,
on hollow stems. Attributed to the Duke of Buckingham's
glasshouse, Greenwich. Circa 1665.

◄PLATE 26   An extremely finely designed and produced
dished *tazza* of unusual size—15 ins. wide, 4 ins. high—and
pattern, in clear soda metal. The tray radially ribbed and
scalloped, the rim folded from above, as is the pedestal foot.
The dish was probably originally gilded. Pre-Ravenscroft,
circa 1670.

PLATE 27 An unblemished example of a sealed Ravenscroft posset pot in uncrizzled lead metal, water-white and lustrous. Cylindrical bowl heavily gadrooned at base, medium kick under, solid handles, the base of the spout bearing the raven's head seal. Height to rim $3\frac{1}{4}$ ins., to top of spout $3\frac{1}{2}$ ins., diameter of rim $3\frac{3}{8}$ ins. Circa 1677.

PLATE 28 Fine goblet bearing the engraved arms of William III, and probably made for his accession. Circa 1689–90.

▶

PLATE 29 Fine *tazza* of the Ravenscroft era in lead metal, lightly crizzled, the bowl with folded rim, ribs in high relief below, on a hollow-pedestal folded foot. Circa 1675.

PLATES 30 & 31 *Left*: Wineglass with lipped round funnel bowl heavily ribbed at base, set on a collar and flattish knop over almost an inverted baluster-type stem. Wide folded foot. Single flint metal, late 17th century. *Right*: Wineglass in brownish-tinted soda metal, the conical bowl fluted at base and 'dimpled' above, collared under, the stem dissected by two adjoining knops. Plain conical foot. Circa 1675.

PLATE 32 *Left*: Tall goblet in lead glass, round funnel bowl heavily gadrooned at base on a serpentine figure-of-eight stem with denticulations. Folded foot. Hawley Bishopp period, circa 1685. *Right*: Bell, heavily 'nipt diamond waies', knopped handle with ring finial. Late 17th century.

PLATE 33 A very fine rare early wineglass showing the Venetian influence, the round funnel bowl trailed and with spiked ribs, supported on a cushion knop with eight pincered wings over a teared dumb-bell knop, terminating in a folded conical foot. $5\frac{1}{4}$ ins. high. Late 17th century.

PLATE 34　Large rummer, the globular bowl 'nipt diamond waies' around the base and resting on a vermicular collar above a hollow cylindrical stem decorated with six bold raspberry prunts in relief, terminating in a high conical foot. $10\frac{1}{4}$ ins. high. Circa 1685.

1675-1720: BALUSTER STEMS

The Glass Sellers Company wanted fashions that could compete in price, shape, and decoration with the styles already familiar in stoneware, earthenware, china, and the Venetian glass which was handled by members of the company. Most of all they hoped that glass would become a popular substitute for silver. Vessels were produced in variety and abundance—fruit dishes, syllabub glasses, cruets, bed-urinals, cream basins, jelly glasses, sweetmeats, candlesticks, ribbed water-glasses, and bottles of all types and sizes.

As for drinking-glasses, this was the period of the baluster stem, which, in its early stages, was a solid stem without knops beneath a round funnel or V-shaped bowl, following Greene's later drawings. In 1682, the year in which Hawley Bishopp officially took over Ravenscroft's Savoy glass-house, appeared 'double flint', which involved a double gathering of the metal, in contrast to 'single flint', which was the name applied to the lighter pieces with thinner bowls, feet and folds, sometimes with hollow stems, which were probably made by London glassmakers employing Italian and other foreign workers accustomed to thin working in soda metal. Though the 'double flint' was favoured by the retailers because it was distinctively English and stood a good chance of ousting foreign competition, 'single flint' at less than half the price continued in popularity between 1675 and 1695. Production of lead crystal was by no means restricted to the Savoy glasshouse, for it was being made in Newcastle about 1684, in Bristol and Dublin about 1691 and in Stourbridge not much later.

Glassmakers at the end of the century were very much in favour of the thicker metal and, after an initial period when inverted or baluster stems predominated, they began further to embellish their glasses with various forms of knops which gave them a most pleasing appearance. The most important of these forms, which are single or in combination, are: inverted balusters; wide angular knops; drop knops; annulated knops; cushioned knops; true balusters; acorn knops; cylinder knops; ovoid or egg knops with cyst at base; mushroom knops with knop at base; and simple knopping. Bowls often had solid bases of great depth and were frequently teared. The most usual forms were the conical, round funnel or waisted bowls, while the trumpet, cup, thistle, and bucket bowls appeared more rarely. The feet were usually folded or domed and folded.

PLATE 35 This unique goblet in lead glass, besides revealing the Venetian influence, also incorporates features seen in Ravenscroft and Hawley Bishopp productions. The bowl has a centrally applied ring with pincered and spiked gadrooning below. The stem comprises double collars, two large hollow quatrefoil knops, and double E-scroll wings with pincered trailing. High conical folded foot. Circa 1710.

PLATE 36 An Anglo-Venetian type wineglass. The wide bucket bowl has a folded rim, chain cabling to the body which is gadrooned beneath. Rib-twisted inverted baluster stem and folded foot. Rare. Early 18th century.

PLATE 37 Goblet, the deep round funnel bowl with heavy 'nipt diamond waies' at base and chain cabling over. Around the rim a single flanged thread. The stem has a semi-hollow prunted bulb between collars over a wide annular knop and base knop. Folded foot. $9\frac{1}{2}$ ins. high. Early 18th century.

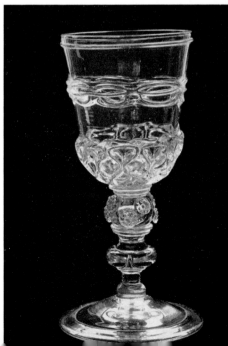

▲ PLATE 38 *Left*: Wineglass, the conical bowl set on a stem with an acorn knop and two collars over a short teared cylinder knop and a teared base knop. Folded foot. 8 ins. high. Circa 1710. *Right*: Wineglass, the ovoid bowl with solid base merging into a wide drop-knop containing an air bubble. Domed and folded foot. 7½ ins. high. Circa 1710.

PLATE 39 Ale glasses of the period are rare and the brew itself was of far greater strength than it is today, so smaller bowls were customary. This specimen has a conical bowl, solid in the base, on a teared acorn-knopped stem and folded foot. 7 ins. high. Circa 1710. ▶

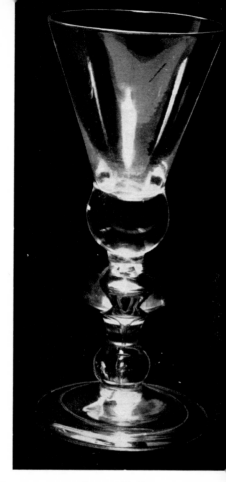

PLATES 40 & 41   Both of these glasses were formerly in the FitzWilliam Museum, and are now in a private collection. *Left*: Wineglass with thistle bowl set on an acorn-knopped stem. Folded foot. 7 ins. high. Circa 1710. *Right*: Wineglass with thistle bowl on a mushroom-knopped stem with base knop. Folded foot. $7\frac{1}{8}$ ins. high. Circa 1710.

PLATES 42 & 43 *Left*: Wineglass with waisted bowl and solid base, the stem comprising a knop followed by a drop-knop over a squat true baluster with a base knop. Foot domed and folded. Very rare combination. Circa 1710. *Centre*: Wineglass with cup-topped round funnel bowl, the hollow tapering stem with an angular knop at top and base knop. High conical folded foot. Single flint with bluish-green tint. Very rare. Circa 1690 to 1700. *Right*: Wineglass with round funnel bowl, solid and teared base, set on an angular knop over a true baluster (both semi-hollow). Conical folded foot. Circa 1715.

PLATE 44 An attractive goblet, the large round funnel bowl slightly solid in the base, set on an impressive cushion knop, small straight section and large base knop (both teared). Conical folded foot. $9\frac{7}{8}$ ins. high. Circa 1700.

PLATE 45 Wineglass, the round funnel bowl with a deep solid teared base on a teared egg-knop stem. Conical folded foot. This type of stem is extremely rare. Circa 1710.

PLATE 46 Goblet, the round funnel bowl engraved with armorials (three *fleur-de-lis*) with date above on a teared squat inverted baluster and teared base knop. Folded foot. 8 ins. high. Circa 1705.

▲ PLATES 47 & 48 *Left*: Goblet, the cup-bowl on a teared inverted baluster stem with knop above and knop at base. High, conical, folded foot. The bowl lightly scratched with the year 1755 (or 1756), but the metal definitely places the glass in the baluster group. 6¾ ins. high. Circa 1720. *Right*: One of a pair of tall marriage goblets, the waisted bowl heavily gadrooned at the base, and with an engraved armorial. Inscribed on reverse *Den 23 April Anno 1724*. Stem with knop over a true baluster and base knop. Plain conical foot. 11½ ins. high. Circa 1720.

PLATE 49 Candlestick in heavy lead metal, the nozzle infolded. The stem comprises a knop and collar over a semi-hollow inverted acorn-knop and a series of collars at the base. Beehive or terrace-type foot. Circa 1710. ▶

PLATE 50   Wineglass, the round funnel bowl solid in the
base, engraved with a facial portrait in diamond-point and
inscribed *J. de Wit* below. The six-sided stem diamond
topped, the foot folded. An English glass with Dutch engraving. $7\frac{1}{2}$ ins high. Circa 1725.

1715–1750: SILESIAN OR MOULDED PEDESTAL STEMS

The accession of George I to the English throne in 1714 is thought to have encouraged the production of this style in England, as it was already well known in Hesse and west Germany. The adoption of the form in England commenced with the four-sided pedestal, in inverted tapering fashion, semi-hollow or with a long tear, and shoulders frequently impressed in relief with a crown, sceptre, or the letters GR. Later the six- and eight-sided pedestal appeared, some with impressed diamonds in relief on the shoulders, and also the twisted or vertically ribbed forms.

Bowls with a collar at the base may be found in all three types of moulded pedestal glass, but collars at the base of the stem are unusual in the four-sided pedestal. In addition to its use in drinking and sweetmeat glasses, the Silesian stem also features in tapersticks and candlesticks. It is usually eight-sided and the right way up in the case of the latter, though the four-sided type also appears occasionally. When there is knopping it is usually in simple form.

The four-sided stems are the rarest, and less than one in ten of all Silesian stem glasses is of the four-sided variety, while the eight-sided are far the most common. These are the main features of the three classifications:

Four-sided: Conical, round funnel, thistle and trumpet-shaped bowls; folded feet.

Six-sided: Conical, round funnel, pan, saucer-topped bucket, thistle and waisted bowls; folded, panel-moulded, domed, domed and folded feet.

Eight-sided: Bowls as above as well as bucket-shaped, cup, ogee, and ovoid bowls, and *tazze* with flat and tray tops; feet as above, though seldom plain.

PLATE 51 Wineglass, the waisted bowl engraved with the arms of the United Netherlands—a lion rampant brandishing in his right paw a curved sword and a conventional representation of thunderbolts in his left. The shield is ensigned with a sovereign's crown and supported by lions rampant. The six-sided stem has an annulated knop at the top, and a knop at the base. Domed foot. An English glass undoubtedly engraved in Holland. 7¾ ins. high. Circa 1720.

PLATE 52 *Left*: Wineglass, similar to that in plate 50, except that it is unengraved. Very rare. 7½ ins. high. Circa 1725. *Right*: Goblet, the cup-bowl gadrooned at the base, on a hollow wrythen knop between collars. Six-sided stem with collar at base. High conical folded foot. 8½ ins high. Circa 1750.

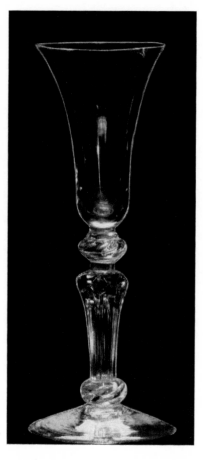

PLATE 53   Ale glass. Bell-bowl with a teared angular knop below, set on a six-sided pedestal stem with diamond-topped shoulders and a teared knop at the base. Plain circular conical foot. $9\frac{1}{8}$ ins. high. Circa 1730.

PLATE 54 Three Newcastle-made Silesian stem glasses, all fine examples of Dutch wheel-engraving. *Left*: Wineglass. Round funnel bowl with the arms of Zeeland. Six-sided stem with a knop at the base, and domed foot. 7¾ ins. high. Circa 1750. *Centre*: Wineglass, engraved with a female figure and *La Bonne Fortune*. The six-sided stem has an annulated knop at the top and collars at the base. Domed and folded foot. 7½ ins. high. Circa 1750. *Right*: Wineglass, bearing a fictitious armorial showing clasped hands within a heart and inscribed *De Geduerige Vrindschap*. The six-sided stem has diamond-topped shoulders and a knop above. Conical folded foot. 6¾ ins. high. Circa 1750.

PLATE 55 Three candlesticks with eight-sided pedestal knopped stems, showing different types of moulded decoration. Circa 1740 to 1750. *Left*: Radially ribbed domed and terraced foot. *Centre*: Socket with short vertical ribs and diamond-moulded domed foot. *Right*: Domed and panel-moulded foot.

PLATE 56 Tall sweetmeat glass, the very shallow bowl having applied loops and prunts. Eight-sided diamond-topped stem with triple collars above and at base. Domed and folded foot which has been broken off and repaired by pegging, as can be distinctly seen. $10\frac{3}{8}$ ins. high. Circa 1750.

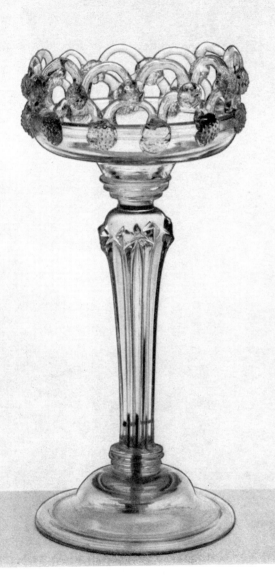

PLATE 57 A Newcastle glass, the round funnel bowl enamelled with a typical Beilby landscape with ruins, and on the reverse an elaborate design featuring foliage, scrollwork, two figures, and a coronet. Signed by Beilby. The stem consists of an angular knop, over a short plain section and another knop, followed almost immediately by a teared central knop. Slightly knopped at base. Conical folded foot. Circa 1765.

1725–1765: BALUSTROID STEMS AND LIGHT BALUSTERS

As the market for glass increased and manufacturers aimed to please the less wealthy, so there was a decline in the quality of the metal used and the flamboyant styles passed away giving place to glasses with smaller bowls and longer stems. This balustroid period (1725–50) includes the 'Kitcat' glasses, named after a type which Kneller depicted the Kitcat Club using to drink a toast. In most cases these will be found with a trumpet bowl on a long, medium, or short baluster stem, in the two latter cases supplemented by medium or long plain sections and occasionally by a base knop. They were considered one of the best types of the period and today make up about one-tenth of the balustroid group. Other features in the same grouping are:

Bucket, cup, ogee, pan, round funnel, trumpet, waisted, ovoid and tray-top bowls, sometimes embellished with ribbing, faint fluting or honeycomb moulding. Inverted baluster or true baluster stems; annulated knops combined with simple knops or an inverted or a true baluster; cylinder, acorn or dumb-bell knops; simple knopping.
Folded, domed, domed and folded and plain feet; also firing feet, and terracing, radial grooving, and ribbing.

The light balusters are better known as 'Newcastle' glasses and with their tall, slender, knopped stems have a far greater appeal than those in the balustroid group. In their period (1735–65) Newcastle had become pre-eminent in the glassmaking industry and had more than 20 glass-houses in operation.

Wheel engravers could get better results on these lead-metal glasses than on the Continental potash-lime specimens, and the elegant Newcastle glasses became very popular with the Dutch engravers especially. Frans Greenwood and Jacob Sang were both important engravers, and later in the century came David Wolff. The leading enamellers were William and Mary Beilby of Newcastle.

Most Newcastle glasses have round funnel bowls, though waisted bowls are quite frequent. Trumpet and conical bowls appear occasionally and cup shapes very rarely. There is a great variety of stems—inverted balusters, true balusters, annulated knops, cushioned knops, mushroom knops, dumb-bell knops, acorn knops, and simple forms with from one to five knops. Feet are plain, folded, domed, or domed and folded.

PLATE 58 *Left*: Newcastle wineglass with waisted bowl, a stem with a teared knop and a plain knop over a semi-hollow inverted baluster with a small knop at the base. Conical foot. $8\frac{1}{8}$ ins. high. Circa 1750. *Right*: Newcastle toasting glass. Trumpet bowl on a slender stem with a central swelling knop. High conical foot. $8\frac{3}{8}$ ins. high. Circa 1750.

PLATE 59 Tall Newcastle goblet. A round funnel bowl on a stem with a flat knop at the top followed by a beaded knop over a slender inverted baluster. Plain foot. Engraved on the reverse of the bowl is the rising sun and *T. Uewaren Van Deeze Bodem*. The sailing vessel has an ensign showing the letters VOC entwined, the initials of the United (Dutch) East India Company (Vereenigde Oost-Indische Compagnie). 9 ins. high. Circa 1750.

PLATE 60   Three wineglasses in soda metal, probably of Belgian (Liège) manufacture, showing the development of the multi-knopped, or bobbin, stem, a style followed in England. *Left:* Waisted bowl with applied short ribs at base. Folded foot. Badly stained brownish colour. The bowl rim is chipped. *Centre:* Waisted bowl with faint vertical moulding. Plain circular foot. *Right:* Waisted bowl with wide ribbed moulding. Plain circular foot. All circa 1720.

PLATE 61 *Left to right*: (1) Goblet with round funnel bowl on a teared inverted baluster stem. Plain foot. Uncommon. Circa 1740. (2) Wineglass with waisted bowl. The stem has a bladed knop and a five-ring annulated knop over a true baluster. Plain foot. Circa 1730. (3) Wineglass with waisted bowl. Teared angular knop in stem. Domed foot. Circa 1740. (4) Goblet or champagne glass with cup-bowl. Central knop and base knop in the stem. The bowl and foot are panel-moulded. Circa 1750.

PLATE 62   Wineglass with trumpet bowl collared at base. The stem contains two annulated knops. The domed and folded foot and bowl are honeycomb-moulded. Annulated knops may have three, five, or seven rings, usually three. A stem with two of these knops combined with the moulded bowl and foot is rare. $6\frac{1}{8}$ ins. high. Circa 1740.

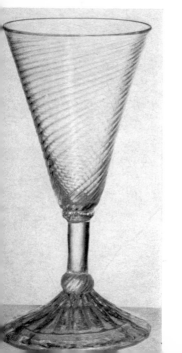

PLATE 63   Wineglass with its deep funnel bowl and knops at top and base of stem all wrythen-moulded. The high conical, folded foot is rib-moulded. 6 ins. high. Circa 1750.

PLATE 64 A mead or low champagne glass, the incurved cup-bowl gadrooned at the base. It has a cushion knop over a semi-hollow stem knopped at top and base. Folded foot. $4\frac{1}{2}$ ins. high. Circa 1750.

PLATE 65 Low champagne glass, the cup-bowl honeycomb-moulded throughout. The stem has an almost central, three-ring annulated knop. Domed and terraced foot. 5 ins. high. Circa 1740.

PLATE 66   Goblet with deep round funnel bowl on a stem with two knops at the top and bottom. Folded foot. The bowl is wheel-engraved with the arms of the Princes of Orange of the House of Nassau. The Arms are ensigned by a Royal Crown. Quarterly: 1 and 4, Nassau; 2 Calzenellenbogen; 3, Vianden; 4, Dietz. An escutcheon in pretence: 1 and 4, Chalon; 2 and 3, Geneva. An escutcheon in chief: Veere. The two additional quarterings in the base, over which is charged the escutcheon of Arkel, are unrecorded by any authority on these arms. $8\frac{3}{4}$ ins. high. Circa 1735.

PLATES 67 & 68 *Left*: Newcastle glass, the round funnel bowl wheel-engraved with the arms of the Bishopric of Utrecht. The stem has an angular knop at the top, a beaded knop near the centre, and a small knop at the base. Folded foot. 7½ ins. high. Circa 1750. *Right*: Wineglass. Round funnel bowl on a collar, the stem with two knops near the top and a small base knop. Conical plain foot. It is not clear whether the inscription *Cherche le Meilleur* refers to the grazing cow or to the owner of the glass. 7 ins. high. Circa 1750.

PLATE 69 Tall goblet, the large round funnel bowl wheel-engraved with a horse over a coronet and on reverse barley ears in saltire. This is the White Horse of Hanover, usually accompanied by the words *George and Liberty*. $8\frac{5}{8}$ ins. high. Circa 1750.

1740–1770: PLAIN STRAIGHT STEMS

This is the largest group of remaining 18th-century drinking glasses. It was a style that could be turned out in profusion for the market that demanded cheapness and quantity rather than quality. These glasses are not very sought-after among collectors, but those who are building up a representative collection of English period glass should not pass them by. There are some attractive and well proportioned trumpet bowls, frequently with teared stems, that are quite common, and there are other rare forms that it would be interesting to discover, like a waisted bucket bowl on anything but a plain foot, an ogee bowl with a teared stem, or an ovoid bowl with a domed or domed and folded foot.

Some of the smaller bowl glasses were made in green-coloured metal, and there are trumpet and waisted bowls in soda metal. Engraving is not generally of a high standard and is mainly composed of flowers, birds, fruiting vines, and hop and barley motifs. Very occasionally there may be faint basal flutes on bucket, cup, and waisted bowls and sometimes on trumpet bowls.

Plain stems may be classified as follows:

Bowls of trumpet, round funnel, waisted, ogee, ovoid, bucket, and cup form.

Straight and plain stems varying in thickness. Toasting stem can be as little as $\frac{1}{8}$ in. in diameter, the semi-toasting stem up to $\frac{1}{4}$ in. The first is rare in lead glass.

Plain or folded feet. Domed or domed and folded feet are rare. Some have flanged, terraced, oversewn, overstrung, or firing feet.

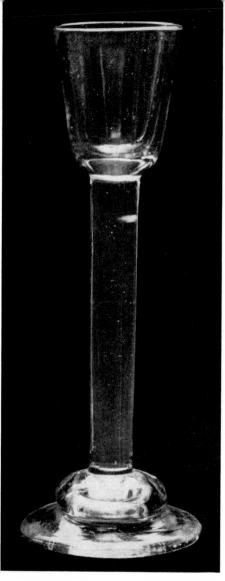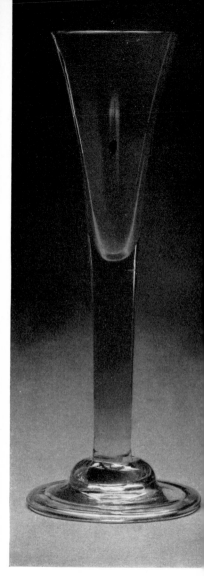

PLATES 70 & 71 *Left*: An Irish cordial glass with round funnel bowl and domed foot. 6¾ ins. high. Circa 1750. *Right*: A tall wineglass with drawn trumpet bowl and domed and folded foot. 8⅜ ins. high. Circa 1750.

PLATE 72 Wineglass with a drawn trumpet bowl, a small
tear in the stem, and a folded foot. Inscribed *Rich: Spurgeon
1746*. Soda metal. An ecclesiastical family of this name lived
in Essex in the mid-18th century, but the name Richard is
not mentioned and it is not certain that this glass was in
their possession. 7 ins. high. Circa 1745.

PLATES 73 & 74 Wineglass with ovoid bowl and plain circular foot. Wheel-engraved on one side with a cannon and on the other with *Loyal Dublin Artillery* and *The Goldsmith's Company*. In the 18th century volunteer regiments were raised locally and many of them were financed privately. This may account for the association with the Goldsmith's Company. 5½ ins. high. Circa 1760.

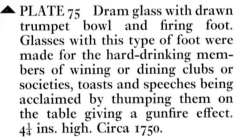 PLATE 75 Dram glass with drawn trumpet bowl and firing foot. Glasses with this type of foot were made for the hard-drinking members of wining or dining clubs or societies, toasts and speeches being acclaimed by thumping them on the table giving a gunfire effect. $4\frac{1}{4}$ ins. high. Circa 1750.

PLATE 76 Dram with ovoid bowl and terraced foot. These small glasses, which, in addition to the firing and terraced feet illustrated, also had plain, folded, flanged, oversewn, or overstrung feet, were principally used for serving the stronger liquors in taverns. $3\frac{3}{8}$ ins. high. Circa 1760.

PLATE 77 *From left to right*: (1) Wineglass with deceptive ovoid bowl and plain foot. Such bowls are of thick glass and hold only a small quantity, though they appear to be of normal capacity. A useful form when one member of the party has to keep a clear head! $4\frac{7}{8}$ ins. high. Circa 1760. (2) Wineglass with ogee bowl and plain foot. $6\frac{3}{8}$ ins. high. Circa 1750. (3) Wineglass with cup-bowl and plain foot. $5\frac{7}{8}$ ins. high. Circa 1750. (4) Wineglass with lipped ogee bowl and plain foot. An unusual bowl form. $6\frac{1}{4}$ ins. high. Circa 1750.

PLATE 78 Cordial glass with waisted bowl and folded foot. Cordials were very potent liquors in the 18th century, and were taken from glasses with small bowls which generally had thick stems to compensate for their height. They are found among nearly all groups of 18th-century glasses. A cordial with this type of bowl on a plain stem is most uncommon. 6¾ ins. high. Circa 1740.

PLATE 79 Wineglass with cup-topped drawn trumpet bowl on a folded foot. This type of bowl is extremely rare. A specimen is known in emerald-green metal with a domed foot. 7 ins. high. Circa 1750.

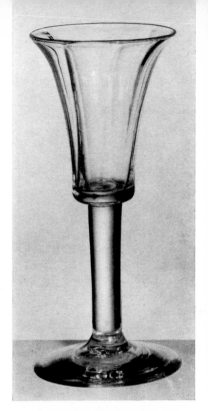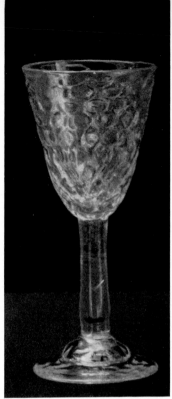

PLATES 80 & 81   *Left*: Wineglass, the waisted bucket-bowl flared and ribbed. Plain foot. The bowl form is extremely rare. 6⅜ ins. high. Circa 1750. *Right*: Wineglass with round funnel bowl on a semi-hollow stem and domed foot. Bowl and foot honeycomb-moulded. 6½ ins. high. Circa 1750.

PLATE 82 *From left to right*: (1) Wineglass, the waisted bowl panel-moulded. Domed and folded foot. $7\frac{1}{4}$ ins. high. Circa 1740. (2) Cordial glass with bell or waisted bowl. Plain conical foot. The stem is thin enough for it to be a toasting glass. $7\frac{1}{2}$ ins. high. Circa 1740. (3) Goblet with bucket bowl and domed and folded foot. Such specimens are rare. $7\frac{1}{4}$ ins. high. Circa. 1750.

PLATE 83   A tall goblet with a drawn trumpet bowl on a
multiple spiral air-twist stem. High conical folded foot.
This is a two-piece glass, that is, the bowl and the stem are
made in one and the foot is added. Multiple spiral air-twist
stems are in the majority in the air-twist series, but the ratio
of the folded foot to the plain foot is about $1:4$. $11\frac{1}{4}$ ins. high.
Circa 1745.

1740-1770: AIR-TWIST STEMS

This category covers about one-seventh of the 18th-century glasses. At first what is known as the multiple spiral twist appeared on the two-piece glasses (bowl and stem made from one gathering of the metal) with straight or simple knopped stems including the ever-popular inverted baluster. Corkscrew twists are found in straight stems. Where the twist continues to run symmetrically into the bowl base the glass is invariably a two-piece. Bowls are principally the trumpet and waisted, feet mainly the plain circular. In the three-piece glasses (bowl, stem, and foot made separately) it was possible to enlarge on the variety of bowls and of twists in the stem. In some specimens (not the multiple spiral) the twist is quite thick and has been aptly termed 'mercurial'.

Two-piece glasses with knopped stems and multiple spiral twist: Trumpet or waisted bowls; inverted baluster stems or one, two, three, or four knops in varied positions; plain feet; domed or folded feet rare.

Two-piece glasses with straight stems: trumpet, waisted, round funnel, cup, bucket, ogee, ovoid bowls; pair of corkscrews, four corkscrews, or multiple-spiral stems; plain, folded, domed, domed and folded feet, occasionally firing feet.

As above with double series twist: trumpet bowls only; two combinations of a vertical column, one or more spiral threads, or single or double corkscrew in stem; plain feet.

Three-piece glasses with knopped stems: multiple spiral or a pair of corkscrews: waisted (or bell), bucket, ogee, round funnel, cup bowls, trumpet very rare; one to five knops in stem in various positions including the angular, annulated, acorn, dumb-bell, inverted and true baluster and collars; plain feet, folded or domed occasionally, domed and folded, firing, or panel-moulded exceptional.

Three-piece glasses with straight stems and single series twist: all bowls previously mentioned; stems are multiple spiral, vertical gauze, one or two spiral gauzes, single or double multi-ply bands, two or four spiral threads, single or double corkscrews, sometimes with collars at bowl or stem base; feet mostly plain, occasionally domed or folded.

Three-piece glasses with straight stems and double series twist: all above bowls except ovoid; stems may have any two from a vertical gauze or column, two or four spiral threads, one or two multi-ply spiral bands, one or two corkscrews; mostly plain feet, a few folded or domed.

PLATE 84 Wineglass with a cup-bowl. The stem has a central swelling knop and contains a double series air-twist: a pair of spiral threads with four spiral threads. (The inner component is always quoted first.) Plain conical foot. Deep emerald colour. 5⅝ ins. high. Circa 1750.

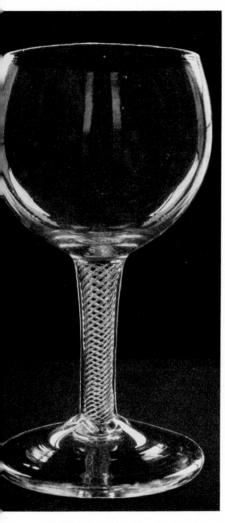

PLATES 85 & 86 *Left*: Goblet with a cup-bowl on a well-formed, multiple spiral air-twist stem and a plain conical (almost semi-domed) foot. A three-piece glass—bowl, stem, and foot are made separately. 8⅛ ins. high. Circa 1750. *Right*: Wineglass. The round funnel bowl has a most unusual moulded decoration. The multiple spiral air-twist stem is composed of an inverted baluster with an angular knop at the centre. Plain conical foot. 6¾ ins. high. Circa 1750.

PLATE 87 *From left to right*: (1) Wineglass with an ogee bowl honeycomb-moulded at the base, the stem containing a spiral cable air-twist. Plain conical foot. 6⅜ ins. high. Circa 1750. (2) Cordial glass with drawn trumpet bowl. The stem has a vertical gauze with four spiral threads. Plain conical foot. 6⅝ ins. high. Circa 1750. (3) Wineglass with round funnel bowl. The multiple spiral air-twist stem has two knops over a slender inverted baluster. 6¾ ins. high. Circa 1750.

PLATE 88 Large wineglass, the ribbed bell-bowl collared ▶ at the base, on an inverted baluster multiple spiral air-twist stem. High conical foot. 7⅞ ins. high. Circa 1750.

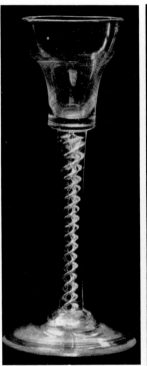

▲ PLATES 89 & 90 Wineglass with a trumpet bowl and a stem containing a single spiral air gauze. Plain conical foot. A three-piece glass—where the bowl joins the stem an abrupt finish to the gauze can be seen. Soda metal. 7 ins. high. Circa 1750. *Right*: Cordial glass with a pan-topped bucket bowl, the stem containing a pair of air corkscrews. High conical foot. 6½ ins. high. Circa 1750.

PLATE 91 Goblet with a bucket bowl. The stem is like that in plate [?], but the corkscrews are more pronounced. A bright and solid twist such as this is sometimes called 'mercurial'. The domed foot makes this glass a rarity. $7\frac{7}{8}$ ins. high. Circa 1750.

PLATE 92 Wineglass with bell-bowl. The multiple spiral air-twist stem has a shoulder knop (almost an inverted baluster), and a vermicular (i.e. ridged) collar in the centre. Plain conical foot. $6\frac{5}{8}$ ins. high. Circa 1750.

▶

PLATE 93 Cider glass, the waisted bowl engraved with the branch of a fruiting apple tree. Multiple spiral air-twist stem with shoulder knop (almost an inverted baluster) and central angular knop. Plain circular foot. $7\frac{1}{2}$ ins. high. Circa 1750.

PLATES 94 & 95   *Left*: Wineglass, the ogee bowl engraved *Loyal Cork Volunteers* within a cartouche. Air-twist stem containing vertical column and four spiral threads. Plain foot. 6¾ ins. high. Circa 1750. Engraving later. *Right*: A 'social' or 'conviviality' wineglass. Round funnel bowl on a multiple spiral air-twist stem, knopped at top and centre. Plain conical foot. The bowl is gilded with the words *Families Friends & Favourites* within a large gilt scroll—possibly the work of the Beilbys. A fine and rare glass of which there is a duplicate in the Victoria and Albert Museum. 7 ins. high. Circa 1760.

PLATE 96 Two Newcastle wineglasses with round funnel
bowls engraved with coats of arms. The stems have a multiple spiral air-twist upper section with central swelling
knop, a teared knop, and a plain lower section with a base
knop. Plain conical feet. *Left*: The pontil is marked *J. Sang
1760*. Jacob Sang was outstanding among the Dutch wheel-
engravers of Newcastle glasses, and signed and dated speci-
mens between 1752 and 1762. $7\frac{3}{4}$ ins. high. *Right*: $7\frac{5}{8}$ ins. high.
Circa 1760.

1740–1770: COMPOSITE STEMS

This section comprises glasses which combine features drawn from plain, air-twist, and opaque twist styles. The group is not large and makes up less than two per cent of the remaining 18th-century glasses. The multiple spiral air-twist and plain stem is the most common, but an air spiral gauze and a pair of corkscrews have appeared. Stems containing an opaque white twist are not common, while combinations of plain, air-twist, and opaque twist are very rare, as are mixed twists with a plain section. Wines outnumber goblets by approximately five to one, ales by twelve to one; only two champagnes and one cordial have been recorded.

The design of these glasses is most attractive, the quality of the metal extremely good, and Newcastle is hardly in dispute as their source. There is very little engraving, and there are few moulded bowls. These are the important styles:

Trumpet, waisted and round funnel bowls are the most common, while the cup. ogee, ovoid, bucket, and pan are very rare.

Stems may have a plain section above an air-twist inverted baluster, or with additional simple knopping or collars, or with simple knopping or collars only; an air-twist over a plain inverted baluster, perhaps with additional knopping or collars, or with knopping or collars only; a plain section over an opaque white twist knopped at top or base or both; an opaque white over a plain inverted baluster; an air-twist knop or plain knop over an opaque white section with two knops; a mixed-twist section set into a plain squat inverted baluster.

Feet may be plain or domed or, rarely, domed and folded. No folded feet have been recorded.

PLATES 97 & 98 *Left*: A very rare candlestick. The nozzle is collared at the base. The stem has a beaded knop over a short plain section, then a shoulder-knopped multiple spiral air-twist section, collared at the base on another beaded knop. Plain domed foot with slight terracing. $10\frac{3}{4}$ ins. high. Circa 1760. *Right*: Goblet with ovoid bowl. The stem has an opaque white twist section over a squat inverted teared baluster. Plain domed foot. $7\frac{1}{2}$ ins. high. Circa 1765.

PLATES 99 & 100 *Left*: Wineglass. Trumpet bowl with solid base on a teared knop. Stem is a multiple spiral air-twist inverted baluster. Plain foot. 6½ ins. high. Circa 1760. *Right*: Wineglass, its round funnel bowl on a straight multiple spiral air-twist section over a squat teared inverted baluster. Domed foot. 6½ ins. high. Circa 1760.

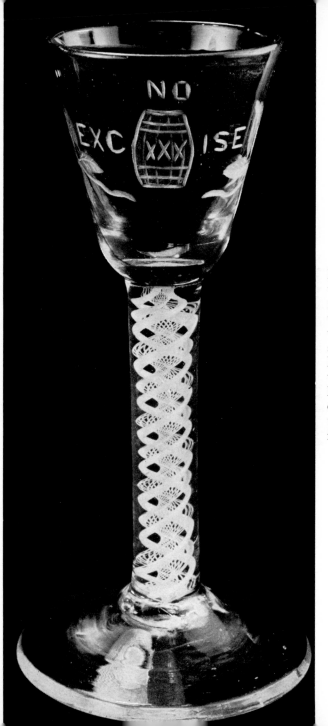

PLATE 101 Larg
wineglass, the roun
funnel bowl engrave
with a barrel and th
words *No Excise* an
a fruiting apple tre
Double series opaqu
white twist stem:
lace twist and a pai
of spiral tapes. Ver
thick conical foot. 7
ins. high. Circa 1760.

1750–1780: OPAQUE WHITE TWIST STEMS

The success of the air-twist stem glasses no doubt encouraged the glass-makers to experiment with white and coloured canes, but the technique had been known since the 16th century when the Venetians revived a much earlier Roman style termed *latticinio* or filigree. The section covers just over one-quarter of the 18th-century glasses, and at least 80 variations of twist have been recorded, either singly or in two's, the former called 'single series'. the latter 'double series'. Three combinations exist, but are extremely rare, as are many of the twists themselves.

Nearly all types of vessel appear and with a variety of bowl formations, but the ratio of unknopped to knopped stems is nine to one. The single series precede the double and triple in date. Bowl decoration is mainly confined to faint moulded basal fluting or simple engraving, but some of Beilby's best work in enamelling is found on opaques. The 'Lynn' glasses (supposed to have originated in that part of Norfolk) with up to seven horizontal rings on the bowl invariably have white twist stems. There is little gilding.

Bowls are usually of bell, round funnel, ogee, pan, trumpet, bucket, ovoid, or cup type, with waisted or saucer-, pan-, or cup-topped variations. Stems may be classified into: one to four knops in various positions; unknopped straight; multiple spiral, vertical and spiral gauzes; one to four and eight spiral threads or tapes; multi-ply spiral bands; lace; corkscrews; spiral tubes; vertical column. Feet are generally plain, seldom folded. Domed or domed and folded are extremely rare. The firing foot, terracing, and radial grooving appears mainly on drams.

PLATES 102 & 103 Bucket and ogee bowls were much used by William and Mary Beilby for their enamel decoration. The pastoral and outdoor scenes date from the mid-1770's when Mary was old enough to assist her brother. *Left*: Goblet, the bucket bowl decorated by the Beilbys. Double series opaque white twist stem: a pair of spiral threads and a pair of multi-ply spiral bands. Plain foot. 6½ ins. high. Circa 1770. *Right*: Wineglass, the ogee bowl enamelled by the Beilbys. Double series opaque white twist stem: a lace twist and a pair of spiral threads. Plain foot. 6 ins. high. Circa 1770.

PLATES 104 & 105   *Left*: Goblet, the bucket bowl enamelled by the Beilbys in white with the coat of a branch of
the Lambton family and elaborate mantling in pink. The
rim is gilded. Double series opaque white twist stem: a
lace twist and a pair of spiral threads. Conical foot. 6⅞ ins.
high. Circa 1770. *Right*: Tall goblet, the ogee bowl wheel-
engraved with masonic symbols within elaborate scrollwork.
Double series opaque twist stem: a vertical gauze and a
pair of spiral tapes. The conical foot is engraved with
flowers. 9⅜ ins. high. Circa 1760.

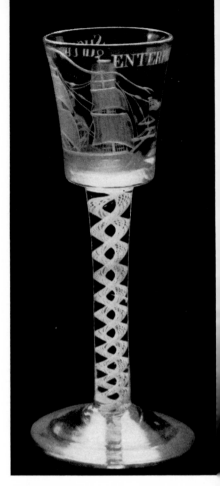

PLATES 106 & 107 *Left*: Large wineglass, the round funnel
bowl engraved with a Dutch bedroom scene and the words
Welkom Twyfelaar. Double series opaque white twist
knopped stem: a lace twist and a pair of spiral threads.
Plain foot. 8 ins. high. Circa 1760. *Right*: Wineglass, the
bucket bowl engraved with a sailing vessel and *Success to
the Enterprise*. Single series opaque white twist stem: a
pair of spiral gauzes. Plain conical foot. A large number of
privateer vessels were sent out to prey on French shipping
during the wars with France in the middle of the century,
particularly from Bristol, and some of the notable ships
were commemorated on glasses of this type. 6½ ins. high.
Circa 1760.

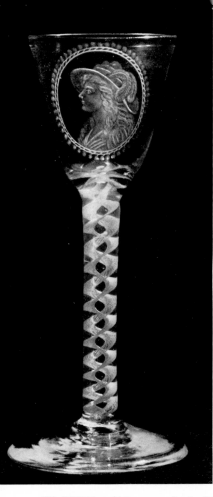
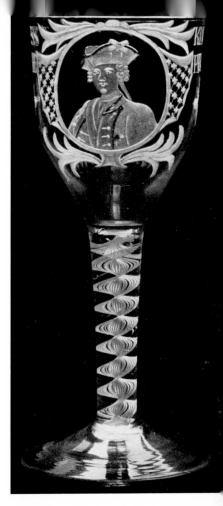

PLATES 108 & 109 *Left*: Wineglass, the round funnel bowl
wheel-engraved with a portrait of an unidentified lady.
Single series opaque white twist stem: a spiral gauze and
a corkscrew entwined. (In the double series twist, there must
be two components, one within the other. The proportion
of the single to the double series in opaque twists is 1:4.)
5¾ ins. high. Circa 1750. *Right*: Goblet, the ogee bowl wheel-
engraved with a portrait of Frederick the Great. Inscribed
Success to the King of Prussia and flanked by the Prussian
Eagle. Single series opaque white twist stem: multi-ply
corkscrew. High conical foot. Probably made during the
Seven Years War. 7¾ ins. high. Circa 1760.

PLATE 110 Ale glass, the ogee bowl enamelled in yellow and touches of brown with initials SMH. On reverse, a crest of a horse's head in a washy red-brown and bridled in yellow. The stem contains a double series opaque white twist: a lace twist and a pair of nine-ply spiral bands. Plain circular foot. Probably the crest of the Horsey or Horsfall family. 7¾ ins. high. Circa 1760.

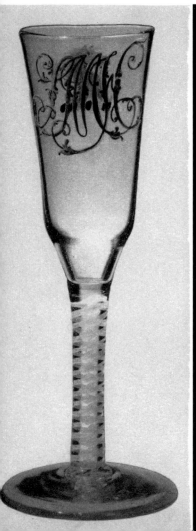
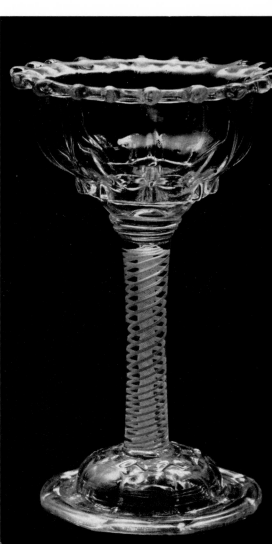

PLATE 112 Sweetmeat glass, the pan-topped bowl with folded rim and applied loops and prunts, collared at base. The double series opaque white twist stem has a lace twist and a pair of spiral threads. Panel-moulded domed foot. $6\frac{3}{8}$ ins. high. Circa 1760.

▶

◀PLATE 111 Sweetmeat glass, the bowl panel-moulded and with a fringed rim, collared at base. Double series opaque white twist stem: a vertical gauze and four spiral threads. The domed and folded foot is also panel-moulded. Panel moulding was much used on sweetmeat and champagne glasses in this period. $6\frac{7}{8}$ ins. high. Circa 1760.

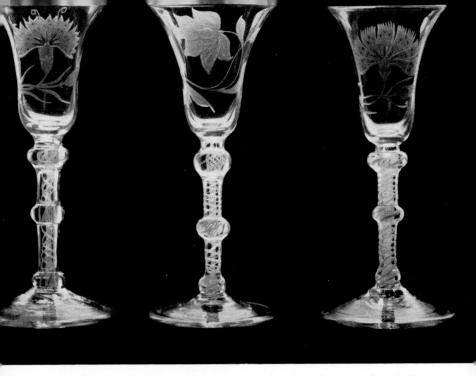

PLATE 113 Three triple knopped wineglasses, the bell bowls wheel-engraved with flower decoration. Double series opaque white twist stems: a vertical gauze and spiral threads. Plain conical feet. *Left & Centre* 6¾ ins. high. *Right* 6⅝ ins. high. All circa 1760.

PLATES 114, 115 & 116 *Top*: A most unusual wineglass, ▶ the cup-bowl with a hollow prunted cylindrical knop at base, the stem containing a multi-ply corkscrew, the foot domed. Bowl, knop and foot are in pale emerald metal. 5½ ins. high. Circa 1760. *Centre*: Rare deceptive ale glass. Double series opaque white twist stem: a pair of spiral tapes and a single, close, multi-ply spiral band. Plain conical foot. 7¼ ins. high. Circa 1760. *Bottom*: Rare gin glass, the ribbed, round funnel bowl with engraved, hatched festoon border. Double series opaque white twist stem: pair of spiral threads and single, multi-ply spiral band. Terraced foot. 4 ins. high. Circa 1760.

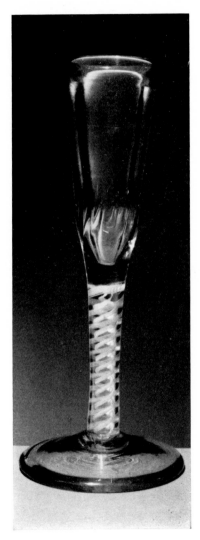

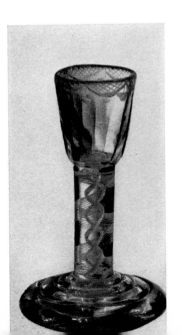

PLATE 117 Wineglass, the round funnel bowl engraved with a portrait of the Young Pretender. Diamond-faceted stem and plain conical foot. This must be one of the latest glasses in the Jacobite series. Circa 1780.

JACOBITE AND
WILLIAMITE GLASS

Many kinds of glasses with Jacobite emblems are known—goblets, wines, cordials, single-handled jelly glasses. All kinds of bowl shape are known, with the possible exception of the ovoid, and all kinds of foot forms, though all but the plain foot are scarce.

Emblems: rose with six, seven, or eight petals, usually six; one or two buds—on the six-petalled rose two buds appear at least twice as often as one; star, oakleaf, thistle, butterfly (or moth), caterpillars, grubs, carnation, daffodil, forget-me-not, honeysuckle, lily-of-the-valley, sunflower.

Mottos: *Audentior Ibo, Fiat, Redeat, Success to the Society.* The latter two are rare. Other Latin mottos are seldom seen.

The mid-18th century seems to have been the period when most specimens of Williamite glasses were produced, probably to celebrate the fiftieth anniversary of William III's defeat of James II's Franco-Irish forces at the Battle of the Boyne, July 1, 1690. The most common type has the equestrian portrait inscribed with a reference to the Boyne and a few words from the Orange Lodges' toast, such as *The Glorious Memory of King William III*, or *To the Glorious and Immortal Memory of King William*. The Ulster Museum, Belfast, among its large collection, has one of the finest specimens bearing the lengthy toast *The Glorious and Immortal Memory of King William and His Queen Mary and Perpetual Disappointment to the Pope the Pretender and all the Enemies of the Protestant Religion*. The Irish harp occasionally appears, but quite a number of glasses have a few words of inscription only.

Vessel forms: trumpet bowls on plain or air-twist stems; waisted on collared and inverted baluster stem; waisted on plain or air-twist stems; bucket and round found on plain stems; ovoid and cup bowl rummers on knopped stems; mallet decanters; jugs with globular-shaped bases.

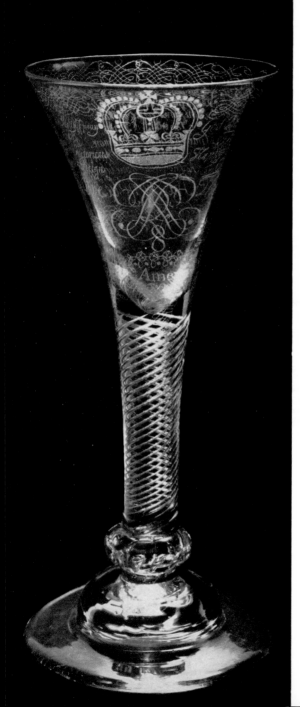

PLATES 118 & 119 Bot
sides of one of the very ra
'Amen' glasses. Goblet wit
a drawn trumpet bowl on
multiple spiral air-twist ste
with beaded knop at bas
Domed foot. The bowl is e
graved in diamond-point wit
two verses of the Jacobi
'anthem', the cipher IR, di
ect and reversed, and th
figure 8, surmounted by
crown. At the base of the bov
the word 'Amen'. Circa 175
Here is the 'anthem' in full:

God Save the King, I pray,
God Bliss the King, I pray,
    God Save the King.
Send Him Victorious,
Happy and Glorious,
Soon to reign over us,
    God Save the King.

God Bliss the subjects all,
And save both great and small
    in every station,
That will bring home the King
Who has best right to reign,
    It is the only thing
    Can save the Nation.

God Bliss the Prince of Wales,
The true born Prince of Wales,
    Sent us by Thee.
Grant us one favour more
The King for to restore
As Thou has done before.
    The familie.

God Save the Church, I pray,
And Bliss the Church, I pray,
    Pure to remain,
Against all Heresie
And Whigs Hypocrisie,
Who strive maliciously
    Her to defame.

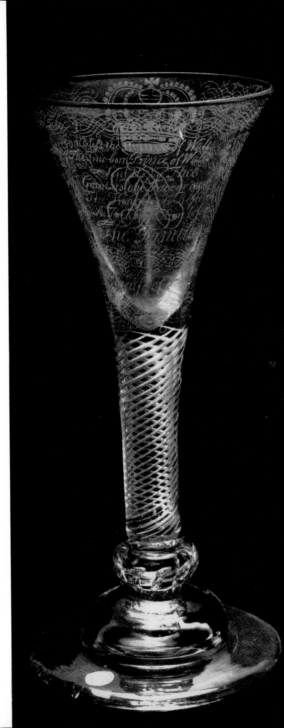

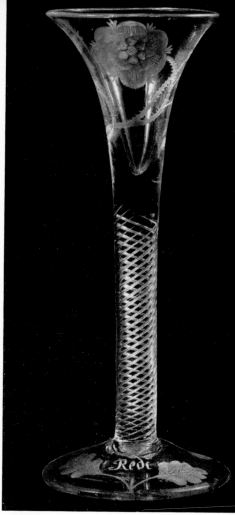

PLATES 120 & 121 *Left*: Wineglass, with drawn waisted bowl on a multiple spiral air-twist stem and folded foot. The bowl engraved with a six-petal rose with one bud and the word *Redeat* in script above. On reverse, a separate thistle, two leaves and a star. 6⅜ ins. high. Circa 1740. *Right*: Wineglass with drawn trumpet bowl on multiple spiral air-twist stem and conical foot. The bowl engraved with a Jacobite rose and two buds, the foot surface with two oak leaves and *Redi*. Presumably a relic of the Oak Society. 6 ins. high. Circa 1740.

PLATE 122   Wineglass, the drawn trumpet bowl on a multiple spiral air-twist. Conical foot. The bowl is engraved with
oak leaf, star, and *Fiat*. On reverse, the Jacobite rose and two
buds. 'Fiat' glasses are attributed to the 'Cycle Club'. 7 ins.
high. Circa 1740.

PLATE 124 Goblet with ogee bowl on centre-knopped, multiple spiral opaque white twist stem. Plain foot. The initials (IFS) are those of James Francis Edward Stuart. The three crowns and the rose blossoms stand for the triple throne he claimed. The oak leaf symbolises mourning. This glass made on the death of the Old Pretender in 1766. ▶

PLATE 123 Three wineglasses with round funnel bowls. *Left*: Bowl with a portrait of Prince Charles Edward and *Audentior Ibo* above, Jacobite rose and buds on reverse. Multiple spiral air-twist stem with two knops. Foot engraved with thistle and leaves. Circa 1750. *Centre*: Bowl engraved with rose and two buds; on reverse, *Fiat* and an oak leaf. Plain stem. Foot showing Prince of Wales's feathers. Circa 1740. *Right*: Bowl engraved with rose and two buds; on reverse, a star. Multiple spiral air-twist stem. Oak leaf on foot. Circa 1740.

PLATE 125 Wineglass, with straight-sided bowl and teared solid base, set on a flat knop and a Silesian eight-sided stem. Folded foot. The Old Pretender is represented by a stricken tree and his two sons by the young oak trees in full leaf on each side. The embracing plant on the tree and the inscription within the ribbon—*Ie Meur ou Ie Matache*—convey the sentiment 'Loyalty or Death'. Very rare to find the motto in French. 7 ins. high. Glass 1715-20. Engraving circa 1735-40.

PLATE 126 Goblet with round funnel bowl on a plain stem and conical foot. The bowl is engraved with an equestrian portrait and inscribed *Y Glorious & Immortal Memory of King William* within a floral circuit. 8 ins. high. Circa 1740.

PLATE 127 Goblet, with drawn trumpet bowl on a multiple spiral air-twist stem and plain foot. The bowl engraved with shamrock border and a broad band of fruiting vine. Inscribed *The Glorious and Immortal Memory of King William III.* $6\frac{5}{8}$ ins. high. Circa 1750.

PLATE 128 Toasting claret jug, the rim engraved with a floral circuit and the body with the inscription *The Glorious Memory of King William that Routed the Irish and French Armie at the Boyne the First July 169*. Four jugs are known in this series, all very similar in shape and size, but the spacing of the inscription varies. English or Irish manufacture. $6\frac{1}{2}$ ins. high. 1760–85.

PLATE 129 Wineglass, the ogee bowl engraved with the name *U C Lange* and date 1779 surmounted by a coronet within a cartouche. On reverse, *J Lange* within a similar cartouche. The stem contains a single grey thread, a pair of canary threads, and a single five-ply opaque white band. High conical plain foot. 7¼ ins. high. Circa 1775.

1755–1775: MIXED AND COLOURED TWIST STEMS

Only about one in forty of the 18th-century glasses fall into these categories, and the mixed twist occurs a little less frequently than the coloured. Canary, purple and emerald green colours are much prized by collectors, though most bright colours attract buyers. Some of the blues, greens, pinks, rubies, and rubber-reds lack intensity of colour. Despite the small number of glasses still extant the variety of combinations is extensive, especially in the soda glasses. All the regular types of bowl appear, the bell and funnel leading the way, but decoration is very rare.

The stem classification is as follows: **air and opaque white**: straight stems, vertical or spiral air gauze or column; opaque white spiral gauze, one, two or four spiral threads; one or four corkscrews; **opaque white and air**: straight stems; opaque white gauze, vertical column or corkscrew; two spiral air threads, spiral gauze, multiple spiral twist; **air and colour**: straight stems; spiral air gauze; single green, blue, or blue and red spirals; **opaque white and colour**: one, two, or three knop stems; opaque white gauze, spiral gauze, lace, spiral threads, corkscrews, cables and bands; edged purple, green, ruby, blue; threads of blue, green, ruby, red, rubber-red, grey-blue, canary, carmine, pink, orange; **air and opaque white and colour**: straight stems; spiral air gauze, opaque white spiral, orange spiral; opaque white vertical thread, spiral air gauze, blue spiral.

Feet are mostly plain, though a few cordials have domed feet, and a mixed-twist wine has a folded foot. Some trumpet drams have firing feet. There are bell, bucket, round funnel, trumpet or flute, ogee, and ovoid bowls.

PLATE 130 *Left*: Wineglass with a trumpet bowl, the stem containing a single vertical blue thread and an opaque white multi-ply corkscrew, edged blue. Plain foot. 6½ ins. high. Circa 1765. *Right*: Ale glass with round funnel bowl, the stem containing a blue gauze and a pair of opaque white multi-ply spiral bands. Plain foot. 7½ ins. high. Circa 1765.

PLATE 131 *Left*: Wineglass, with bell-bowl, the stem containing an opaque white spiral gauze together with one
rubber-red, one green, and one white spiral thread. Plain
foot. 6½ ins. high. Circa 1765. *Right*: Wineglass with bell-
bowl, the stem containing confused spiral air threads
(possibly accidental), one ruby and one blue spiral thread,
and a pair of multi-ply opaque white corkscrews. Plain
conical foot. 7 ins. high. Circa 1765.

PLATE 132 An imposing and rare goblet, the cup-bowl engraved with a Japanese garden scene and two figures, the base bridge-fluted. The stem has six vertical flutes, and a central knop with cut relief diamonds. The domed, scalloped foot is scale cut. 9¾ ins. high. Circa 1780.

1760–1800: FACETED STEMS

The majority of these glasses are two-piece—the cutting of the stem extends into the bowl base, which is not possible with three-piece glasses, and is known as 'bridge-fluting'. Diamond- or hexagonal-shaped facets were the favourites, the first being thought the earlier, but vertical fluting, spade- and scale-cutting were also employed. There are nearly always six facets to a circuit though occasionally seven can be found.

As the century advanced there was a tendency towards smaller bowls on drinking glasses, and the majority of facet stems have round funnel, ogee, or ovoid bowls. Sometimes the cutting makes it difficult to distinguish between the last two types. Engraved decoration, composed of conventional stars with alternate ovals or circles perhaps linked with festoons, is a common feature of the rim borders and occasionally appears on the bowl base. There are some glasses with larger bowls, stippled in the manner of David Wolff, if not by the master himself, and there are ale glasses decorated with the hop and barley motif. Basal fluting and other forms of cut or moulded bowl decoration are scarce. Stem knopping consists mainly of the central swelling knop or a knop at the top. The feet may have scalloped or petal-cut rims, or be radially fluted.

Bowls: round funnel, ogee and ovoid; occasional trumpet or waisted forms, other forms seldom; an octagonal round funnel has been known.

Stems: diamond, hexagonal, or vertical (sometimes notched) flutes; scale- or spade-cut; unknopped or with top or central knop or central swelling knop.

Feet: plain, with fluting, scalloping or petal-cutting, other forms rare; folded, domed or firing exceptional; domed and folded unknown.

PLATE 133 *Left*: Wineglass, the round funnel bowl bridge fluted, the upper part with cut ovals and so-called 'stars'. The centre-knopped stem is cut with diamond facets. Plain circular foot. $5\frac{1}{2}$ ins. high. 1770–80. *Centre*: Wineglass, the ogee bowl bridge-fluted. Stars and circles on the rim. The diamond-cut stem is centrally knopped. Plain circular foot. $5\frac{3}{8}$ ins. high. 1770–80. *Right*: Wineglass, the ovoid bowl bridge-fluted. Centrally-knopped, diamond-cut stem. The foot is diamond cut, giving a shaped edge. $5\frac{7}{8}$ ins. high. 1770–80.

PLATES 134 & 135 *Left*: Rare dram glass. The rim of the ovoid bowl is engraved with stars and circles. The stem is bridge fluted and diamond faceted. Plain circular foot. $4\frac{3}{8}$ ins. high. Circa 1780. *Right*: Goblet, the diamond-moulded cup-bowl is on a hexagonal faceted stem. Plain circular foot. Goblets with this type of bowl are far from common. $6\frac{3}{4}$ ins. high. Circa 1780.

PLATE 136 Ale glass, the bowl engraved with stars and circles. Diamond-faceted stem and plain conical foot. Ale glasses of this type are found quite frequently in this series, but the rather similar ratafia glasses with narrower bowls are much rarer. $6\frac{3}{4}$ ins. high. Circa 1770.

PLATE 137 *Left*: Wineglass, the round funnel bowl bridge-fluted on a diamond-faceted stem. The domed foot makes the glass rare. 5½ ins. high. Circa 1770. *Centre*: Wineglass, the ovoid bowl bridge-fluted and inscribed *Bona Fide* within a floral cartouche, the rim with short vertical flutes. Diamond-faceted stem and plain circular foot. 5¼ ins. high. Circa 1770. *Right*: Wineglass, the unusual-shaped bowl bridge-fluted and engraved with floral decoration. Diamond-faceted stem and plain circular foot. 6 ins. high. Circa 1770.

PLATE 138 *Left*: Decanter, three triple rings on the fluted neck, upper part of body with a band of cross-cut diamonds centrally starred, at base a band of alternate wide short flutes and fine diamonds. Polished pontil. Mushroom stopper. Circa 1820. *Right*: Decanter with two triple rings on a partly fluted neck, upper part of barrel-shaped body with a band of alternate cross-cut diamonds and fine diamonds and lozenges, between two relief rings and two pairs of rings (above and below). Slanting blazes on base and polished pontil. Mushroom stopper. Circa 1820.

IRISH AND CUT GLASS

The imposition of the Excise tax on glass in England in 1745 forced the glassmaker to work in lighter metal and to use only simple cut decoration, such as shallow fluting or stars, except on the stems of glasses, where facet cutting could be used.

By transferring their activities to Ireland, where the Excise duty was not imposed until 1825, the glass manufacturers could produce thicker glass vessels which gave more scope to the cutter. But though much of the finely cut glass of the late 18th and early 19th centuries is attributed to Ireland, it seems that England continued to be an important producer of cut glass thanks to the revived popularity of the style.

The thicker the glass, the more elaborate the design could be. The star frequently found on the base of vessels was enlarged from six to more than 20 points. Decanters and bottles had prisms, diamonds and hobnails on their bodies and stoppers, and there were shell or fan patterns on the rims of bowls and dishes.

Among the many items of cut glass will be found butter dishes or coolers, finger bowls, salt cellars, salad bowls (canoe-shaped or with turn-over rims), water jugs, decanters, wine glasses (rummers in particular) and chandeliers. The decanters are highly sought after, especially if they bear on their bases the mark of the Cork Glass Company, Penrose Waterford, Waterloo Co. Cork or Waterford Co. Cork.

With the coming of moulded imitations in the 1850's cut glass was eclipsed for a few decades, but it returned to favour during the last quarter of the 19th century, both in England and America, and has maintained its position ever since.

PLATE 139 Irish salad bowl, the turned-over rim having a centre band of diamonds and half-diamonds between short flutes. Base of the bowl with ovals and the plain stem with a centre knop. Ribbed domed foot on a square solid base. $8\frac{3}{8}$ ins. high. $10\frac{1}{4}$ ins. diameter. Late 18th century.

PLATE 140 Irish salad bowl, the turned-over rim cut with vertical flutes, the bowl cut with diamonds between semi-ovals, on three legs. This type is the forerunner of that in plate 139, and its form is probably derived from mid-18th-century objects in silver. $5\frac{7}{8}$ ins. high. $7\frac{3}{8}$ ins. diameter. Circa 1775.

◄PLATE 141 Circular salad bowl with fan-cut rim and the body cut with fine diamonds on a plain centrally-knopped stem and radially-cut foot. 8 ins. high. 8¾ ins. diameter. Circa 1820.

PLATE 142 *Left*: Jug with serrated rim also horizontally fluted, the upper part of the body cut with wide flat flutes, the lower part with fine diamonds. 7⅝ ins. high. Circa 1820. *Right*: Pitcher-shaped jug with cut rim, the upper part of the body cut with fine diamonds, the lower part vertically fluted. Radially-cut foot. 9½ ins. high. Circa 1800.

PLATE 143 *Left*: A two-piece moulded celery vase with turn-over rim. It shows plainly the difference between moulded and genuinely hand-cut glass when compared with the jug on the right. Irish, probably Cork. 6½ ins. high. Circa 1830. *Right*: Jug, finely cut all over with various designs – diamonds, flutes, scalloping, semi-ovals, and triangles. The glasscutter meant to show off his artistry on this one. 7½ ins. high. Circa 1800.

PLATE 144 *Left*: An Irish sugar bowl, the protruding rim with short flutes, the body with relief diamonds. Wide flutes at base on a domed foot with a square moulded base. Circa 1820. *Right*: An Irish goblet, the cup-topped bucket bowl cut with stars, flutes, and other motifs. Short collared and flattish-knopped stem, and square moulded base. Early 19th century.

PLATE 145   A handsome pair of table-lights, with lemon-coloured drops, on black and white Wedgwood bases ormolu mounted. 13 ins. high. Early 19th century.

PLATE 146 One of a pair of two-light candelabra with pineapple-shaped finial and cut diamonds in the stem and branch-holders. Four-pillared stand, ormolu-mounted at base. 27½ ins. high. Circa 1800.

PLATE 147 Irish decanters. *Left*: Three triple-rings to neck, shoulders fluted, the barrel-shaped body cut with arches, diamonds, and stars. Fluted base. Mushroom stopper. 8 ins. to lip. Circa 1820. *Centre*: A variation of the cutting in the left-hand decanter. Mushroom stopper. $7\frac{3}{4}$ ins. to lip. Circa 1820. *Right*: Two triple rings on the neck, the shoulders cut with four bands of circles, the body with geometrical cutting. Tall flutes at base. Fluted target stopper. $8\frac{1}{2}$ ins. to lip. Circa 1820.

PLATE 148 *Left*: Plain decanter with three triple rings to neck, the body faintly fluted at base, target (bull's eye) stopper. *Waterloo Co Cork* impressed under base. Circa 1820. *Centre*: Small plain decanter with two single rings on the neck, the body faintly fluted at base, plain disc stopper. *Edwards Belfast* impressed under base. Circa 1800. *Right*: Plain glass decanter with three double-milled rings and faintly moulded at base of body. Fluted target stopper. *Cork Glass Co* impressed under base. Circa 1800.

PLATE 149 *Left*: Tall decanter of amethyst colour, the neck cut with rings, the body with wide flutes at top and base. Spire stopper. Polished concave base. Circa 1840. *Right*: Long-necked decanter with bulbous body in clear glass flashed with green. Spire stopper. Circa 1850.

PLATE 150 *Left*: Tall decanter of a pale green colour, the neck and spire stopper facet-cut, the body with pillar moulding. 12¾ ins. high. Circa 1830. *Right*: Decanter in deep emerald green glass, wholly cut with diamond facets. Stopper with metal mount. 9½ ins. to lip. Circa 1830.

PLATE 151 *Left*: Three Bristol Blue condiment bottles with slice-cut pear stoppers in a silver-plated stand. *Centre*: A set of Bristol Blue decanters with pear-shaped stoppers. The decanters have gilded labels for Brandy, Rum, and Hollands (gin) and are shown in their original Regency black laquer stand which has a brass handle, supports, and feet. *Right*: Bristol Blue condiment bottle labelled in gilt *Essence of Lemon*.

NAILSEA AND BRISTOL

Nailsea, near Bristol, has had its name applied to a type of glassware in a rural style made mostly in bottle glass splashed with colour or opaque white. Some of the earliest of this type was made in bottle-making glasshouses farther afield, as Nailsea itself was a crown glass factory. This glass was taxed at a much lower rate, and its cheapness and colourfulness kept it high in popularity from 1780 to 1830 after which it became displaced by the moulded or pressed plain glass. But production continued throughout the century and a revival occurred at the end of the century when coloured pipes, bells, and walking-sticks were turned out in profusion. Among the better-known objects in Nailsea are the jugs, bottles, mugs, and flasks, and novelty items included walking-sticks, rolling-pins, pipes, bells, shoes, hats, and bellows.

Many consider that the outstanding production of the Bristol industry is Bristol Blue, though opaque white, bright green, and clear cut glass was also made in the area. Gilding, enamelling in colours and engraving were all of a high standard by the beginning of the 19th century. Nearly all kinds of vessel were made—decanters, cruet bottles, salt cellars, wineglasses, tumblers, finger bowls, tea caddies, toilet bottles, and vases.

PLATE 152 Bristol wineglasses, their colours varying from peacock blue to dark green. There are trumpet, bucket, and ovoid bowls and a variety of knops in the stems in the front row. All the glasses are heavy and set firmly on their shaped bases.

PLATE 153 *From left to right*: (1) Dark blue Bristol flagon with a metal ball stopper and a metal cap over the neck. Strap handle. (2) A flat onion-shaped decanter with a ringed lip and a mother-of-pearl stopper. (3) A boot-glass. Named after Lord Bute, the much-disliked landlord and politician. The toast would be drunk to 'Down the boot'. (4) Light blue Bristol flagon with a metal stopper in the form of a grape-vine and a strap handle. The neck is capped with a metal cover.

PLATE 154 Four Bristol condiment bottles in dark blue glass decorated and labelled in gilt, with facet-cut stoppers. It will be noticed that the stopper in the third from the left differs from the other three. It probably replaces a broken original. The bottle shape closely follows that of the decanters in plate 155/2 & 3. Late 18th century.

PLATE 155 *Left to right*: (1) Decanter in dark blue glass with three bladed rings to the neck and lozenge stopper. Decorated and labelled in gilt. Circa 1800. (2) & (3) Pair of spirit decanters in emerald-green glass with lozenge stoppers. Decorated in gilt with urns suspended on chains and labelling. Shrub was a drink or cordial now rarely found. It was generally made of currant juice boiled with sugar and water to which some spirit, usually rum, was added. Both early 19th century.

PLATE 156 Opaque white candlestick, the incised twist shaft with collars at top and bottom, the candle-socket and domed foot with enamelled floral decoration. This type of painting is typical of the work executed by Michael Edkins, and by his son and staff, during the second half of the 18th century. $9\frac{1}{2}$ ins. high. Circa 1780.

PLATE 157 *Left*: Cream jug and sugar basin in opaque white glass decorated in red, blue, and green with black rims. Jug $4\frac{1}{2}$ ins. high. Basin $4\frac{7}{8}$ ins. high. Circa 1800. *Centre*: Sugar basin in milk-white glass inscribed in gilt. $4\frac{7}{8}$ ins. high. Circa 1800. *Right*: Cream jug and sugar basin in opalescent white glass, decorated in red, green, and brown. Jug 4 ins. high. Basin $4\frac{3}{4}$ ins. high. Circa 1800.

PLATE 158 Two Nailsea jugs in bottle-green glass splashed with white. Typical examples of the Nailsea style, though they could have been made elsewhere. *Left*: 9⅛ ins. high. *Right*: 8¾ ins. high. Early 19th century.

PLATE 159   The use of an ultra-violet lamp to discover
whether glass is of lead or soda is only possible when the
glass is clear. *Left*: Flask in clear soda-glass, splashed with
red and a little blue. 8¾ ins. high. Circa 1820. *Right*: Bottle
in clear lead-glass splashed with red and blue. 9½ ins. high.
Circa 1820.

PLATE 160 These specimens in the Stourbridge Collection are known as 'friggers' – fancy objects to show off the
glass maker's versatility. They were very popular during
the first three decades and the final decades of the 19th
century. In addition to hats and small bellow-shaped flasks,
glassmakers made tobacco-pipes, walking-sticks, and rolling-pins in blue glass, opaque white glass, or clear glass
with *latticinio* decoration. 19th century.

PLATE 161   *Left*: Jug in bottle-green glass with white
wrythening. 6½ ins. high. Early 19th century. *Centre*: Bottle
in brownish-green glass flecked with white, with applied lip
ring. 6½ ins. high. Early 19th century. *Right*: Jug in bottle-
green glass sparsely flecked with white. 6¼ ins. high. Early
19th century.

PLATE 162 Large rummer (or Goblet), the cup bowl collared at base on a square lemon-squeezer foot. The bowl is
wheel-engraved *Sunderland Bridge* (opened 1796), and depicts
the bridge and sailing vessels. The number of lamps on
these glasses (here seven) vary from five to eleven. For
reverse see plate 171. Circa 1800.

LATE EIGHTEENTH AND EARLY NINETEENTH CENTURY GLASS

Jelly Glasses: These were first made during the early 18th century in the heavier lead metal of that period with conical or waisted bowls, some gadrooned at the base, stems consisting mainly of a knop, and feet that were plain, folded, domed, or domed and folded. Later in the century, diamond-moulded, panel-moulded, ribbed, and wide fluted bowls appeared in addition to the plain bowl, and bowl forms themselves extended in range though the metal became thinner and of less pleasing appearance.

Dwarf Ale Glasses: Those with bowls having some form of heavy gadrooning, short stems with pinched wings or of propellor type, and folded feet are commonly attributed to the 17th century, but some of the later 18th-century glasses also have these features and only the quality of the metal can distinguish them. But bowl decoration is also more diverse, including wrythening or ribbing, wide basal fluting, and engraved hop and barley motifs.

Rummers: This type of glass with a largish bowl on a short stem—the name is derived from the German *roemer*—began to appear about the middle of the 18th century and became popular in the 1770's. With their large bowl surface they were eminently suited to the art of the engraver. Bowl decoration otherwise is confined to wide moulded flutes seldom going more than halfway from the base. There are more than a dozen forms, in spite of the short stems, and the plain circular foot outweighs the square foot by roughly four to one.

Georgian Wines: These are mostly small glasses, in form following that of the rummers and probably made between 1770 and 1830. Wide basal fluting on the bowls is the principal form of decoration.

Monteiths: Also known as 'bonnet glasses', probably used for salt, confectionery, or the like, and date from about 1760. Bowl decoration includes diamond-moulding, basal flutes, and frequently a blue rim, on a petal or scalloped foot. Some are wholly in blue glass. A later style with cut bowls and square feet continued well into the 19th century.

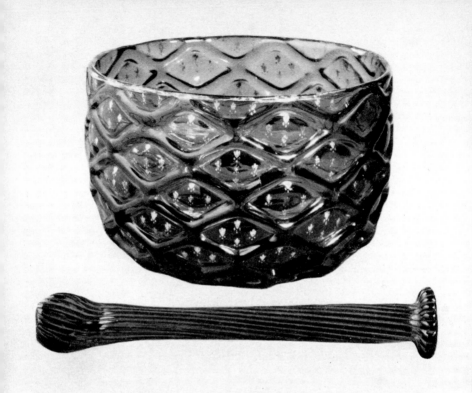

▲ PLATE 163   Finger bowl in brilliant green metal, diamond-moulded and with gilded decoration of heraldic ermine design. Also, an incised sugar-crusher in green metal. Bowl 3 ins. high and 4½ ins. wide. Circa 1830.

PLATE 164   *Left*: Monteith in amethyst-colour metal with moulded bowl. 2⅜ ins. high. Circa 1800. *Centre*: Miniature decanter in amethyst-colour glass with plain and ringed neck and diamond-moulded style body. Probably a copy of a very early decanter. 5 ins. high. Circa 1800. *Right*: Monteith in blue glass, dimple-moulded, and with petal foot. 2⅞ ins. high. Circa 1800.

PLATE 165   *Left*: Sugar basin in blue glass with cut flat ▶ diamonds and star base. Silver-mounted rim. 3⅝ ins. high, 4⅞ ins. wide. Circa 1810. *Right*: Sugar basin in blue glass, vertically fluted and notched, with petal-cut foot and silver rim and handle. Crested with an engraved pair of arms holding cross crosslets. 3⅞ ins. wide, 4½ ins. high. Circa 1810.

PLATE 166   Three jugs in soda metal, all early 19th century. *Left*: Plain glass with two applied rings, swan-neck type handle and ring foot. 11¼ ins. high. *Centre*: Swirling flutes to body. 8⅜ ins. high. *Right*: Body vertically fluted. 6½ ins. high.

PLATE 167   Glass jug engraved with the badge of Ireland– ▶ a crown above a harp – the latter flanked by the date 1782. A motto *In Pectore Patria* in capitals in ribbon over, *Lisburn Volunteers* in very bold capitals around base of body. 7¾ ins. high. Circa 1782.

PLATE 168 A pair of rummers with ovoid/ogee bowls collared at base on short plain stems with large cysts (or half-knops). Plain circular feet. The bowls are engraved with Yarmouth Church and the arms of Yarmouth. Circa 1810.

PLATE 169 William Absolon of Great Yarmouth was an enameller and gilder on glass during the late 18th and early 19th century, but there is no evidence that he was also an engraver. However, the work on these glasses was no doubt done in the same part of the country. *Left*: Barrel-shaped tumbler engraved and gilded with the monogram AB and *A Trifle from Yarmouth* above. On reverse a wheatsheaf within an oval medallion flanked by two ears of barley and the words *May farming flourish.* $4\frac{1}{4}$ ins. high. Early 19th century. *Centre*: Rummer with ovoid/ogee bowl on a domed square foot, the bowl engraved with the initials WS within a wreath. On reverse, the arms of Norwich. $5\frac{3}{4}$ ins. high. Early 19th century. *Right*: Tumbler, fluted at base, engraved with the arms of Yarmouth. On reverse, the initials DBS. $4\frac{1}{8}$ ins. high. Early 19th century.

▲ PLATE 170 Pair of rummers with ovoid bowls on four-
sided pedestal stems and solid square feet. The bowls are
acid-etched, one with a woodland cottage scene, the other
with an interior showing two men returning from the shoot
and on its reverse, two men game-shooting. Acid-etching
was not seriously developed in this country until the mid-
19th century, so the decoration can be assumed to be much
later than the glasses. 6¼ ins. high. Early 19th century.

PLATE 172   Tumbler engraved with a sailing vessel and
the words *To Nelson the Brave Hero of the Nile.* On reverse
God Save the King above a crown and GR cipher, flanked by
the initials WS, all in the same bold capital lettering. 4 ins.
high. Circa 1800.

PLATE 173 Rummer with ovoid/ogee bowl collared at base, short plain stem with cyst, and plain circular foot. The bowl rim engraved with stars and ovals and below, in very bold capital letters, *May the Wings of Frendship Never Loose a Fether*. On reverse, the monogram TT in a circle. Sometimes called a 'social glass'. $5\frac{3}{4}$ ins. high. Early 19th century.

PLATE 174 *Left*: Rummer with bucket bowl on a double capstan stem and plain circular foot. Engraved *Queen Caroline* for the supporters of the ill-used Queen of George IV. 5 ins. high. Circa 1820. *Right*: Rummer, the bucket bowl engraved with an equestrian portrait of the King's Champion glove in hand. On reverse, the Royal Crown and *G IV R July 19 1821*. A coronation glass for George IV. $5\frac{1}{8}$ ins. high.

PLATE 175 *Left*: Short ale glass, the bowl engraved with hop and barley ears and inscribed *May Health and Peace Flow all Around and Love Sincere with Bliss be Crownd*. Initials NS and date 1776. Engraving later than the glass. $5\frac{7}{8}$ ins. high. *Right*: Rummer with bucket bowl on a spreading, partly ribbed stem and square solid foot. Engraving shows a Royal Mail coach. Inscription: *How Sweet the Love that Meets Return—Health to the Sick Honor to the Brave—Success to the Lover and Freedom to the Slave*. 6 ins. high. Early 19th century.

PLATE 176 *Left*: Rummer with bucket bowl on double capstan stem. Engraved with arms of Blacksmith's Company and *By Hammer and Hand all Arts Do Stand*. A 'trade' glass. $5\frac{1}{2}$ ins. high. *Right*: Tumbler fluted at base engraved with the hop vine and *The Hop Trade*. $4\frac{1}{4}$ ins. high. Both early 19th century.

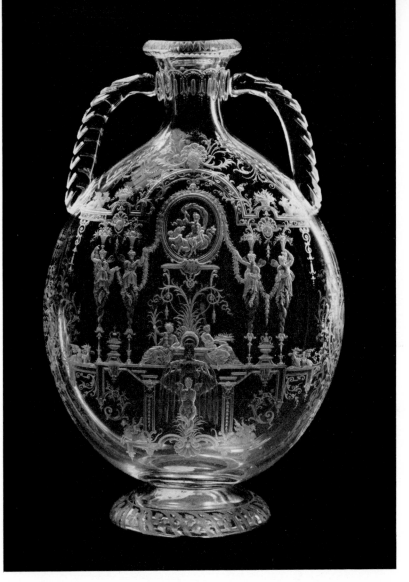

PLATE 177 A magnificently engraved two-handled vase.
Engraved in capital letters under the foot: *Exhibited by W.
T. Copeland & Sons 160 New Bond Street 1873 – Design
Arranged by J. Jones – Engraved by P. Oppitz.* The exhibition
was in Vienna. Paul Oppitz was a well-known engraver of
the period and J. Jones an artist employed by Copelands.
$11\frac{1}{8}$ ins. high.

VICTORIAN GLASS

The repeal of the Excise Act in 1845, the introduction of press moulding from America, and the development of an automatic process for
bottle making gave a new impetus to glass production to the delight of
the less affluent who could now obtain glass for their own homes at
reasonable prices. But high-quality glass was also produced.

After 1819, Apsley Pellatt manufactured 'sulphides'—small white
paste figures or portraits which were usually overlaid by clear glass—by
a technique formerly used in France. These cameos may be found in
drinking vessels, decanters, toilet bottles and paperweights.

Coloured glass, which was already popular in Bohemia, became
fashionable in England just before the Great Exhibition of 1851. At
the Exhibition the exhibitors' lists advertised objects in black, blue,
brown, green, pink, purple, ruby, red, yellow and jewel-stone colours.

Roman cameo glass also aroused interest, and in the 1860's John
Northwood turned his attention to this difficult process. Some of the
early pieces took several years to complete, but by the '80's production
on a commercial scale had become possible, and the leading names in
this style were Stevens & Williams, (where John Northwood was the
art director), and Thomas Webb, with which George Woodall was
associated. The style attracted some American interest and a few Stourbridge artists emigrated to do similar work there.

Other decorative techniques included wheel-engraving, acid-etching,
painting, gilding and silvering. There is an increasing demand for early
Victorian glass now that the 'hundred year rule' has brought it within
the antique period.

PLATE 178 *Centre*: Single-handled English decanter in amethyst-coloured glass. 8¾ ins. high. Late 19th century. *Right*: English decanter with applied rings to neck, also in amethyst-coloured glass. 8½ ins. high. Late 19th century. Compare with *left*, a two-handled Venetian decanter in clear glass. 9⅛ ins. high. Early 20th century.

PLATE 179 Wine flagon and stopper, the body engraved ▶ with a Roman soldier in a four-horse chariot. Possibly from a Stourbridge glasshouse. 12⅝ ins. high. Circa 1860.

▲ PLATE 180   Three similar-shaped scent bottles with different cutting and stoppers, all clearly impressed *Pellatt & Co. Patentees* below the portrait medallions. *Left*: Adelaide, wife of William IV. Circa 1830. *Centre*: Lord Brougham. Circa 1820. *Right*: Marked *W IV R* Circa 1830.

PLATE 181   Cut-glass scent bottle with spire stopper inset with a cameo of the head of Gladstone. $7\frac{1}{2}$ ins. high. Mid-19th century.

PLATE 182 English paper-weight, the floral design produced by the use of coloured canes embedded in thick colourless glass which magnifies the pattern. In England they were sold in stationers' shops. Mid-19th century.

PLATE 183 Small squat cameo vase, with dark red background and a design of flowers and foliage in relief cut from the overlaid opaque white glass. Late 19th century.

PLATE 184 Tall glass beaker engraved on the wheel in relief and intaglio ('rock crystal' engraving). Designed by and executed under William Fritsche for the New York Trades Fair. Fritsche had his own workshop at Thomas Webb's factory in Stourbridge. Circa 1900.

PLATE 185   Glass vase engraved on the wheel by the Bo-
hemian Frederick E. Kny, who was associated with Thomas
Webb at Stourbridge from the 1860's until late in the century.
Circa 1880.

PLATES 186 & 187 *Left*: Both sides of a tall wine bottle in deep amber glass, decorated with chip-work engraving, and bearing a moulded manufacturer's mark, *Sachs & Hochheimer Frankfurt*, around the base. The tree fish and bird are taken from the arms of Glasgow. 13¾ ins. high. Circa 1878. *Right*: Both sides of a globular bottle in green glass decorated with chip-work engraving. Base marked WGL within an escutcheon. This method of engraving was a speciality of the Alloa Glass Works, and the building could well be meant to represent the factory. Circa 1849.

PLATES 188 & 189 Large flagon of flat, oval shape with a single handle, engraved with a representation of Alexandra Palace with the gardens in the foreground. On the handles in small capitals *Engd by F. Eisert*. He was listed in 1885 as Franz Eisert, glass engraver, 25 South Audley Street, London. The flagon was reproduced in the *Illustrated London News*, October 19 1872: 'The handsome claret jug presented to the Lord Mayor . . . When the vendors can be assured that £100,000 will be forthcoming they will enter into a contract for sale . . . The Lord Mayor was sure this could be raised and with his friends signed the deeds . . .'

PLATES 190 & 191 *Left*: Goblet in white opaline glass, transfer-printed in black with an ass. On reverse a man drinking. Gilded rim. Exterior matt finished. Base marked *Richardson's Vitrified* and *16th April*. The firm of W. H., B. & J. Richardson of Stourbridge was one of the leading manufacturers in the Midlands. 6⅝ ins. high. Mid-19th century. *Right*: Vase with ivory tone. The globular body carved in light relief with passion flowers, prunus blossom, and a butterfly. Impressed on base *Thomas Webb & Sons*. Cameo glass. 12¼ ins. high. Late 19th century.

PLATE 192   Ewer, transfer-printed in black with three views of an Eastern water-carrier (only one seen in photo). Matt finish. Rim and back of handle gilded. Base marked *Richardson's Vitrified* and the date *6th July 1847*. 9¼ ins. high.

PLATE 193   Amber-coloured champagne glass, the bowl profusely engraved with floral decoration. Foot of the same colour. The plain stem six-sided. Late 19th century.

PLATE 195   Handled custard glass in lead metal with ▶ lipped cup-bowl on a single series opaque white twist stem. Plain circular foot. The twist is very poor compared with the 18th-century twists. Late 19th century.

PLATE 194 *Left*: Goblet, the round funnel bowl engraved with flowers and berries, the stem following the style of the eight-sided pedestal stems of the early 18th century. $7\frac{1}{8}$ ins. high. Circa 1880. *Right*: Goblet, the U-shaped bowl engraved with floral decoration, the stem cut and following the pattern of a collared and inverted baluster of the early 18th century. $7\frac{3}{4}$ ins. high. Circa 1880.

PLATE 196 Tumbler engraved in diamond-point with three coats of arms, the date 1851, and some verses. Perhaps made for the Great Exhibition, and the verses added later. 4¾ ins. high.

PLATE 197 Goblet, the bowl engraved with fruit, foliage,
and geometrical and other designs, on a cut six-sided stem
and circular foot. Signed under bowl base *W. Fritsche.*
$5\frac{7}{8}$ ins. high. Late 19th century.

PLATE 198 The high optical quality of British full lead-crystal glass give it a fascinating versatility. It may either be decorated – and each type of decoration seems to give it a changed character – or it may base its appeal on a smooth shape and on the inner glow from the glass itself. These two sherry glasses have each a beaded bubble, not 'winking at the brim', but trapped in the depth of the bowl, and a gracefully blown hollow base. The great beauty of the brandy balloon is in its shape and in the astonishing thinness of its walls. Decanter and glasses by Whitefriars Glass Ltd. Brandy balloon by Thomas Webb & Sons. 20th century.

MODERN GLASS

The simple design of the glasses Philip Webb made for William Morris in 1859, and the accent placed on variety in the metal by Christopher Dresser in the latter half of the 19th century, have both had an important influence on 20th century glass production. The English glass industry, which has passed through a serious crisis in this century due to the competition of new industrial materials, has also struggled to find a style suited to the 20th century and has been too often tempted to copy slavishly the elegant designs of the 18th century. But the last few years have seen an extraordinary resurgence in the glass industry. The conviction that with cut-crystal glassmakers could do nothing but emulate the old designs has been finally destroyed by the modern cut crystal produced by Webb Corbett from designs by David Queensbury, Professor of Ceramics at the Royal College of Art. Whitefriars, who have long produced elegant and beautifully designed glass after the manner of Philip Webb, have now moved on, under new designers such as Geoffrey Baxter and Martin Newman, to produce many original ideas about texture, shape and colour. What is even more heartening is that new factories are being founded. In Devon, a new generation of glassmakers is to be trained by Swedish glassmen, and the factory that is to begin in a similar way in Caithness is now successfully producing a simple range of glasses and vases in blues and greys and browns.

Those who seek 20th century glasses whose monetary value is likely to increase rapidly, however, will probably turn to the commemorative glass. Examples of this include mugs or glasses commemorating Edward VIII's abdication, vessels recalling George VI's and Elizabeth II's coronations, and the piece in honour of the RAF's success in the Battle of Britain, inscribed with Churchill's memorable words.

PLATE 199 Goblet, the waisted bowl engraved and gilded, the bulb stem enclosing a silver 1916 threepenny piece. Made to commemorate the death of Lord Kitchener during the Great War. On reverse, the inscription *His Work was Done ere we could Thank Him*. Almost 10 ins. high.

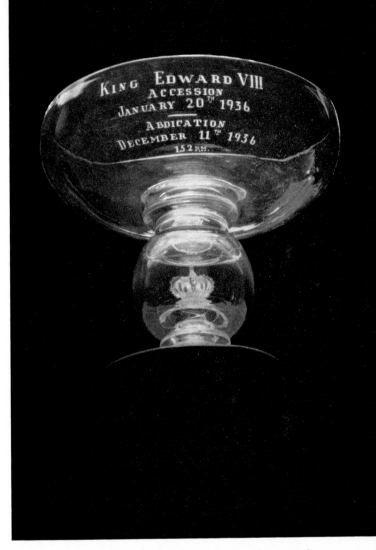

PLATE 200 *Tazza* commemorating the accession and abdication of King Edward VIII. The bowl base contains a silver token and the stem bulb a glass model of a crown. One of an edition of 50 numbered glasses made to the order of Thomas Goode & Sons. $4\frac{7}{8}$ ins. high. $5\frac{1}{4}$ ins. diameter.

PLATE 201 Vase of cylindrical shape (in cinnamon, indigo, or willow coloured glass) with rugged surface texture. Designed by G. P. Baxter for Whitefriars Glass.

PLATE 202 *Foreground*: Two diabolo-shaped vases (in amethyst midnight blue or sea green). *Background*: Three vases, two of them keg-shaped, the larger in midnight blue and the smaller in amethyst. Made by Whitefriars Glass.

PLATE 203 The real delight of these glasses is in the chiaroscuro effect of their texture. An outer casing of lead-crystal gives a feeling of remote clarity to the colours. Casing is done by gathering one glass on top of the other and blowing and working them as one.

PLATE 204 Hand-made vase with rippled surface and swirls ▶ of green or brown. Designed by W. J. Wilson for Whitefriars Glass. Made in three sizes: 7 ins., 9 ins., or 10 ins. high. 1964.

PLATE 205   Hand-made vase (in arctic blue or twilight-coloured glass) designed by W. J. Wilson for Whitefriars Glass. 8 ins. high.

PLATE 206   Vase designed by Irene M. Stevens for Webb ▶ Corbett of Stourbridge. 14 ins. high.

INDEX

Plate numbers are shown in bold face type

Index

Index

Index

Index

Index